I0411851

September 2014

CONSUMER FINANCIAL PROTECTION BUREAU

Some Privacy and Security Procedures for Data Collections Should Continue Being Enhanced

CONSUMER FINANCIAL PROTECTION BUREAU

Some Privacy and Security Procedures for Data Collections Should Continue Being Enhanced

GAO
Highlights

Highlights of GAO-14-758, a report to congressional addressees

Why GAO Did This Study

Congress created CFPB in 2010 as an independent agency to regulate the provision of consumer financial products and services, such as mortgages and student loans. CFPB has begun collecting consumer financial data from banks, credit unions, payday lenders, and other institutions. GAO was mandated to examine CFPB's collection of consumer financial data. This report addresses (1) the scope, purposes, uses, and authorities of CFPB consumer financial data collections and (2) CFPB's compliance with laws and federal requirements, including government-wide privacy and information security requirements.

GAO reviewed laws, regulations, and contracts pertaining to CFPB's data collections; reviewed privacy and information security policies; reviewed inspector general reports on CFPB's information security program; assessed how CFPB applied NIST's framework for managing risks of storing data; examined access controls on the system maintaining consumer financial data; and interviewed CFPB and other regulatory officials, privacy experts, and representatives from randomly selected financial institutions.

What GAO Recommends

GAO makes 11 recommendations to enhance CFPB's privacy and information security and 1 recommendation to OCC to ensure its data collections comply with appropriate disclosure requirements. CFPB and OCC agreed with GAO's recommendations and noted steps they plan to take or have taken to address them.

View GAO-14-758. For more information, contact A. Nicole Clowers, 202-512-8678, clowersa@gao.gov.

What GAO Found

To carry out its statutory responsibilities, the Consumer Financial Protection Bureau (CFPB) has collected consumer financial data on credit card accounts, mortgage loans, and other products through one-time or ongoing collections. As the following table shows, these large-scale data collections varied from about 11,000 consumer arbitration case records from a trade association to 173 million mortgage loans from a data aggregator. Of the 12 large-scale collections GAO reviewed, 3 included information that identified individual consumers, but CFPB staff indicated that those 3 were not subject to statutory restrictions on collecting such information. Other regulators, such as the Board of Governors of the Federal Reserve System (Federal Reserve) and the Office of the Comptroller of the Currency (OCC), collect similarly large amounts of data.

CFPB has taken steps to protect and secure these data collections. For example, it created a data intake process that brings together staff with relevant expertise to consider the statutory, privacy, and information security implications of proposed consumer financial data collections. CFPB staff described a process for anonymizing large-scale data collections that directly identify individuals. In addition, CFPB had taken steps to implement an information security program that is consistent with Federal Information Security Management Act requirements, according to the Office of Inspector General for the Federal Reserve and CFPB. GAO found that CFPB had implemented logical access controls for the information system that maintains the consumer financial data collections and was appropriately scanning for problems or vulnerabilities. CFPB also established a risk-management process for the information system that maintains consumer financial data consistent with guidelines developed by the National Institute of Standards and Technology (NIST).

However, GAO determined that additional efforts are needed in several areas to reduce the risk of improper collection, use, or release of consumer financial data.

- **Written procedures and documentation:** CFPB lacks written procedures and comprehensive documentation for a number of processes, including data intake and information security risk assessments. The lack of written procedures could result in inconsistent application of the established practices. For example, CFPB unnecessarily retained sensitive data in two collections GAO reviewed, but its staff said they plan to remove this information. GAO recommends CFPB establish or enhance written procedures for (1) data intake, including reviews of proposed data collections for compliance with applicable legal requirements and restrictions; (2) anonymizing data; (3) assessing and managing privacy risks; and (4) monitoring and auditing privacy controls; and (5) documenting results of information security risk-assessments consistently and comprehensively.

- **Implementation of privacy and security steps:** CFPB has not yet fully implemented a number of privacy control steps and information security practices, which could hamper the agency's ability to identify and monitor privacy risks and protect consumer financial data. GAO recommends CFPB take or complete action to (1) develop a comprehensive written privacy plan that brings together existing privacy policies and guidance; (2) obtain periodic

_____ United States Government Accountability Office

independent reviews of its privacy practices; (3) develop and implement targeted privacy training for staff responsible for working with sensitive personal information; (4) update remedial action plans to include all identified weaknesses and realistic planned remediation dates that reflect priorities and resources; and (5) include an evaluation of compliance with contract provisions relating to information security in CFPB's review of the service provider that processes consumer financial data on its behalf.

- **Paperwork Reduction Act compliance:** Under the Paperwork Reduction Act (PRA), agencies generally must obtain Office of Management and Budget (OMB) approval when collecting data from 10 or more entities to minimize burden and maximize the practical utility of the information collected. CFPB and OCC collect, on an ongoing basis, credit card data from different

institutions—representing about 87 percent of outstanding credit card balances—and agreed to share data. However, OMB staff said the agencies' collections and data-sharing agreement may warrant OMB review and approval. Additional consultation with OMB regarding these collections and the data-sharing agreement would help both agencies ensure they are fully complying with the law. Furthermore, OCC had not obtained OMB approval for its credit card and mortgage data collections, which each included more than nine entities. Without approval, OCC lacks reasonable assurance that its collections comply with PRA requirements intended to reduce burden. GAO recommends (1) CFPB consult further with OMB about its credit card collection and data-sharing agreement, and (2) OCC seek OMB approval for its credit card and mortgage data collections.

CFPB's Large-Scale Collections of Consumer Financial Data from January 2012 through July 1, 2014

Data collection	Scope	Ongoing or one-time	Contains information that directly identifies individuals?
Arbitration case records: consumer case records from January 2010 through early 2013	11,204 case records	One-time	✓
Automobile sales: vehicle transaction-level data from 46 state motor vehicle departments matched with consumer credit data	700,000 vehicles per month	Ongoing (monthly)	
Consumer credit report information: nationally representative sample panel of consumer credit information	10.7 million individuals	Ongoing (monthly and quarterly)	
Credit cards: individual consumers' credit card account-level data, with linkages to credit reporting data	25-75 million total accounts[a]	Ongoing (monthly)	
Credit scores: random samples of consumer reports and credit scores calculated on such reports	600,000 consumer credit reports	One-time	
Deposit advance products: deposit account and transaction-level data, including use of deposit advance products	100,000-500,000 accounts	One-time	✓[b]
Mortgages: loan-level data from large servicers for mortgages	29 million active loans; 173 million total loans	Ongoing (monthly)	
Online payday loans: loan summaries from a sample of borrower files from online payday lenders, matched with consumer credit data	300,000 borrowers	One-time	
Overdraft fees: account and transaction-level data based on random samples of consumer checking accounts	2 million accounts and related transactions	One-time	
Private-label mortgages: loan-level data on loans packaged into private-label mortgage-backed securities	4 million active loans; 21.9 million total loans	Ongoing (monthly)	
Private student loans: loan-level data on all educational loan originations from 2005 through 2011	5.5 million total loans	One-time	
Storefront payday loans: borrower-level activity for all loans within a period of 12 or more months	15-40 million total loans	One-time	✓[b]

Source: GAO analysis of CFPB information. | GAO-14-758

[a]CFPB has access to credit card data from additional credit card issuers through an information-sharing agreement with the Office of the Comptroller of the Currency, which collects more than 500 million total accounts on a monthly basis. When combined, these data contain information about 87 percent of outstanding credit card balances by volume as of March 2014.

[b]CFPB removed information that directly identifies individuals from the files staff use to analyze these data.

Contents

Figure

Abbreviations

CARD Act	Credit Card Accountability Responsibility and Disclosure Act of 2009
CFPB	Consumer Financial Protection Bureau
CFTC	Commodity Futures Trading Commission
DHS	Department of Homeland Security
FDIC	Federal Deposit Insurance Corporation
FHFA	Federal Housing Finance Agency
FISMA	Federal Information Security Management Act of 2002
FTC	Federal Trade Commission
GSS	general support system
HMDA	Home Mortgage Disclosure Act
MOU	memorandum of understanding
NCUA	National Credit Union Administration
NIST	National Institute of Standards and Technology
OCC	Office of the Comptroller of the Currency
OIG	Office of Inspector General
OMB	Office of Management and Budget
PIA	privacy impact assessment
PRA	Paperwork Reduction Act
SEC	Securities and Exchange Commission
SEFL	Division of Supervision, Enforcement, and Fair Lending
SORN	system of records notice

GAO
U.S. GOVERNMENT ACCOUNTABILITY OFFICE

441 G St. N.W.
Washington, DC 20548

September 22, 2014

Congressional Addressees

The Dodd-Frank Wall Street Reform and Consumer Protection Act (Dodd-Frank Act) created the Bureau of Consumer Financial Protection—also known as the Consumer Financial Protection Bureau (CFPB)—to regulate the offering and provision of consumer financial products or services under the federal consumer financial laws.[1] According to the act, CFPB's mission is to implement and enforce federal consumer financial law consistently to ensure that markets for consumer financial services and products are fair, transparent, and competitive, among other things. The act directs CFPB to carry out its mission by, among other things, collecting, researching, monitoring, and publishing information relevant to the functioning of markets for consumer financial products and services to identify risks to consumers and the proper functioning of such markets. Prior to and during the 2007-2009 financial crisis, we and others noted that the lack of data on consumer financial products and services hindered federal oversight in areas such as mortgages and fair lending.[2]

Since its creation, CFPB has undertaken activities including conducting examinations of financial institutions and taking enforcement actions against various entities. The independent agency also has issued reports on consumer financial issues (credit card markets, student loans, and

---

[1]Pub. L. No. 111-203, § 1011, 124 Stat. 1376, 1964 (2010) (codified at 12 U.S.C. § 5491).

[2]See GAO, *Financial Regulation: A Framework for Crafting and Assessing Proposals to Modernize the Outdated U.S. Financial Regulatory* System, GAO-09-216 (Washington, D.C.: Jan. 8, 2009); *Fair Lending: Data Limitations and the Fragmented U.S. Financial Regulatory Structure Challenge Federal Oversight and Enforcement Efforts*, GAO-09-704 (Washington, D.C.: July 15, 2009); and *Consumer Protection: Federal and State Agencies Face Challenges in Combating Predatory Lending*, GAO-04-280 (Washington, D.C.: Jan. 30, 2004). See also Adam J. Levitin, *The Consumer Financial Protection Agency*, Pew Financial Reform Project Briefing Paper #2 (Georgetown Law Center: 2009); and Subcommittee on Domestic Monetary Policy and Technology, House Committee on Financial Services, *Regulatory Restructuring- Safeguarding Consumer Protection and the Role of the Federal Reserve*, 111th Cong., 1st sess. (July 16, 2009).

GAO-14-758 CFPB Data Collections

consumer credit reports) as required by the Dodd-Frank Act.[3] It also has issued numerous rules required by the act.

To carry out these activities, CFPB has begun collecting consumer financial data—information on individual consumers' financial activity at the account, loan, or transaction level—including information on credit card accounts, credit reporting agency records, and mortgage loans.[4] However, some industry participants and members of Congress have raised questions about the nature and scope of CFPB's data collections, including whether the collections comply with statutory restrictions on CFPB's ability to collect personally identifiable financial information.[5] They also questioned whether the agency has taken sufficient steps to ensure that these data will not be subject to unauthorized disclosure.

We were asked to review CFPB's collection of consumer financial data. Subsequently, the Consolidated Appropriations Act of 2014 mandated us

---

[3]The Credit Card Accountability Responsibility and Disclosure Act of 2009 (CARD Act) originally directed the Board of Governors of the Federal Reserve System (Federal Reserve) to biennially conduct a review, within the limits of its existing resources available for reporting purposes, of the consumer credit card market. Pub. L. No.111-24, § 502(a), 123 Stat. 1734, 1755 (2009). However, the Dodd-Frank Act transferred all consumer financial protection functions of the Federal Reserve to CFPB. Pub. L. No. 111-203, § 1061(b)(1), 124 Stat. at 2036. The Dodd-Frank Act also required CFPB to issue one-time reports on various issues related to private education loans and lenders, and the credit scores sold by consumer reporting agencies. Pub. L. No. 111-203, §§ 1077, 1078, 124 Stat. at 2075-76.

[4]For purposes of this review, we did not examine the consumer financial data CFPB obtains through consumer complaints or through its enforcement activities. The Inspector General for the Federal Reserve and CFPB has conducted several reviews on the consumer complaint database. For example, see Board of Governors of the Federal Reserve System, Consumer Financial Protection Bureau, Office of Inspector General, *Evaluation of the Consumer Financial Protection Bureau's Consumer Response Unit* (Sept. 28, 2012).

[5]We consider personally identifiable financial information to be a subset of consumer financial data. The term "personally identifiable financial information" is not defined in the Dodd-Frank Act, but CFPB has defined it by regulation as any information a consumer provides to a financial institution to obtain a financial product or service from that institution; information about a consumer resulting from any transaction involving a financial product or service between the financial institution and a consumer; or information the financial institution otherwise obtains about a consumer in connection with providing a financial product or service to that consumer. Personally identifiable financial information does not include information that does not identify a consumer, such as aggregate information or blind data that do not contain personal identifiers, such as account numbers, names, or addresses. 12 C.F.R. § 1016.3(q).

to study similar issues.[6] This report examines (1) CFPB's consumer financial data collection efforts, including the scope, purposes, uses, and authorities for these collections, and the extent to which CFPB has collaborated with other federal financial regulators as part of these collections; (2) the extent to which CFPB complied with statutory restrictions on its consumer financial data collection authorities and federal privacy requirements; and (3) the extent to which CFPB has assessed the risks of these collections and applied appropriate information security protections over these data.

To examine the scope, purposes, uses, and authorities for CFPB's consumer financial data collections, we reviewed statutes, regulations, and publications related to consumer financial data collections undertaken by CFPB and the prudential regulators—the Board of Governors of the Federal Reserve System (Federal Reserve), the Office of the Comptroller of the Currency (OCC), the Federal Deposit Insurance Corporation (FDIC), and the National Credit Union Administration (NCUA).[7] We reviewed CFPB and OCC contracts with data aggregators and physically reviewed several of CFPB's data collections on-site. We interviewed officials and staff from CFPB and the prudential regulators. We also discussed the extent to which other agencies with financial markets or consumer regulatory responsibilities collect consumer information. We spoke with staff from the Commodity Futures Trading Commission (CFTC), Consumer Product Safety Commission, Federal

---

[6]Ranking Member Crapo, Committee on Banking, Housing, and Urban Affairs, United States Senate, requested that we examine CFPB's data collection efforts. Chairman Capito, Subcommittee on Financial Institutions and Consumer Credit, and Ranking Member Maloney, Subcommittee on Capital Markets and Government Sponsored Enterprises, Committee on Financial Services, U.S. House of Representatives, subsequently asked us to examine CFPB's and other regulators' data collection efforts. Finally, House Report 113-172 required GAO to examine CFPB's data collection efforts and report to the House and Senate Appropriations Committees within 180 days of the date of enactment of applicable funding legislation for fiscal year 2014, which was the Consolidated Appropriations Act, 2014. Pub. L. No. 113-76, 128 Stat. 5 (2014). This report responds to both requests and the mandate. Furthermore, we briefed relevant committee staff.

[7]We focused our analysis of CFPB's data collections, studies, and examination materials on consumer financial data collections that occurred since January 2012, as CFPB had limited data collections before that time. We reviewed the inclusion of information that directly identifies individuals in the large scale consumer financial data collections of OCC, FDIC, and the Federal Reserve. We did not assess the privacy or information security controls of these collections for this report.

Housing Finance Agency (FHFA), Federal Trade Commission (FTC), and Securities and Exchange Commission (SEC). We also reviewed reports and interviewed staff from organizations that analyzed privacy issues, monitored consumer financial topics, and serve as industry associations for financial institutions.

To examine data collection restrictions and requirements and privacy protections for consumer financial data maintained by CFPB, we compared CFPB's practices against statutory requirements and guidance from the Office of Management and Budget (OMB) and the National Institute of Standards and Technology (NIST). We reviewed CFPB privacy policies and procedures, and interviewed CFPB's Chief Information Officer, Chief Privacy Officer, and other staff about their privacy-related policies, practices, and controls implemented. We discussed CFPB's consumer financial data collections with OMB staff who review federal data collections and compliance with statutory requirements. We also spoke with consumer and privacy advocacy groups about their views on CFPB's consumer financial data collections and with an academic expert about the extent to which data collections containing personal information can be de-anonymized.[8] We took steps to ensure the accuracy of key information used in this report, including interviewing agency officials, obtaining original source documents, and physically observing database contents on-site when necessary, and determined that the information was sufficiently reliable for our purposes.

To examine the extent to which CFPB had assessed the risks of these collections and applied appropriate information security protections, we

---

[8]For purposes of this report, the term "personal information" is used to refer to any information about an individual maintained by an agency, including (1) any information that can be used to distinguish or trace an individual's identity, such as name, Social Security number, date and place of birth, mother's maiden name, or biometric records, and (2) any other information that is linked or linkable to an individual, such as medical, educational, financial, and employment information. Researchers analyzing personal behavior or characteristics using individuals' personal information take steps to mask (anonymize) the identity of individuals in these datasets. This process involves removing identifying characteristics such as name, address, birth date, and Social Security number. Some researchers have raised concerns about the extent to which related individual information in datasets (such as gender and zip code) could allow outside groups or researchers to reveal (de-anonymize) the identities of individuals in the dataset. Throughout this report we use the term "de-anonymize" because it is used in federal privacy guidelines. Other researchers have used "reverse engineer" to describe the same process.

reviewed CFPB's security policies and procedures for systems that store consumer financial data and compared them with applicable NIST guidance and CFPB's own security standards. We interviewed CFPB's Chief Information Officer, Chief Information Security Officer, and other staff about their information security policies, practices, and controls. We also reviewed the logical access controls for the hardware and systems environment CFPB uses to store and analyze consumer financial data.[9] See appendix I for more information about our scope and methodology.

We conducted this performance audit from August 2013 to August 2014 in accordance with generally accepted government auditing standards. Those standards require that we plan and perform the audit to obtain sufficient, appropriate evidence to provide a reasonable basis for our findings and conclusions based on our audit objectives. We believe that the evidence obtained provides a reasonable basis for our findings and conclusions based on our audit objectives.

Background

The Dodd-Frank Act transferred consumer protection oversight and other authorities over certain consumer financial protection laws from multiple federal regulators to CFPB, creating a single federal entity to, among other things, ensure consistent enforcement of federal consumer financial laws.[10] The Dodd-Frank Act charged CFPB with the following responsibilities, among others:

- ensuring that consumers are provided with timely and understandable information to make responsible decisions about financial transactions;

---

[9]Agencies use logical access controls to determine which staff may use which electronic information and systems and what may be done to the information that is accessed. Methods for controlling logical access include requiring a user to enter a password or other identifiers to access information stored on a computer.

[10]These authorities transferred on July 21, 2011. CFPB has supervision and enforcement authority for federal consumer protection laws for depository institutions with over $10 billion in assets and their affiliates. The federal prudential regulators—the Federal Reserve, OCC, FDIC, and NCUA—which previously supervised and examined all depository institutions and credit unions for consumer protection, also retain supervision and enforcement authority for certain consumer protection laws for those depository institutions with over $10 billion in assets and their affiliates. In addition, they continue to supervise institutions for consumer protection that have $10 billion or less in assets.

- ensuring that consumers are protected from unfair, deceptive, or abusive acts and practices, and from discrimination;

- monitoring compliance with federal consumer financial law and taking appropriate enforcement action to address violations;

- identifying and addressing outdated, unnecessary, or unduly burdensome regulations;

- ensuring that federal consumer financial law is enforced consistently, without regard to the status of a person as a depository institution, in order to promote fair competition;

- ensuring that markets for consumer financial products and services operate transparently and efficiently to facilitate access and innovation; and

- conducting financial education programs.

Furthermore, the Dodd-Frank Act gave CFPB supervisory authority over certain nondepository institutions, including certain kinds of mortgage market participants, private student lenders, and payday loan lenders.[11] Such institutions generally lacked federal oversight before the financial crisis of 2007-2009.

CFPB's Data Collection Authorities and Restrictions under the Dodd-Frank Act

The Dodd-Frank Act grants CFPB certain authorities that govern its collection of consumer financial data. The act also includes certain restrictions on CFPB's collection and use of personally identifiable financial information and requirements to ensure that CFPB protects such data. The primary authorities and related restrictions we examined are included in three sections of the act:[12]

---

[11]The Dodd-Frank Act also gave CFPB supervisory authority over "larger participants" in markets for consumer financial products or services as CFPB defines by rule. 12 U.S.C § 5514(a)(1)(B). Title X also contains additional authorities and responsibilities for CFPB that are not outlined here.

[12]The Dodd-Frank Act also provides CFPB with additional authorities to collect consumer financial information, such as to carry out its enforcement and consumer response (complaint) responsibilities, but these authorities are outside the scope of this report.

- **Market monitoring**. Under section 1022(c), CFPB is directed to monitor for risks to consumers in the offering or provision of consumer financial products or services, including developments in consumer financial markets for such products or services, in order to support its rulemaking and other functions. The act provides CFPB with the authority, in conducting such monitoring, to gather information from time to time regarding the organization, business conduct, markets, and activities of covered persons and service providers, from a variety of sources, including several sources specified in the act.[13] Under this data collection authority, CFPB is prohibited from obtaining records from covered persons and service providers participating in consumer financial services markets for the purposes of gathering or analyzing the personally identifiable financial information of consumers.[14]

- **Supervision of nondepository covered persons**. Section 1024 provides CFPB with the authority to supervise entities (other than depository institutions or insured credit unions) that provide certain consumer financial products or services.[15] This authority also extends to service providers.[16] In addition to assessing the extent to which these entities comply with federal consumer financial laws and obtaining information about their activities and compliance systems or procedures, this section charges CFPB with requiring reports and conducting examinations of the nondepository persons the section covers for purposes of detecting and assessing associated risks to consumers and markets for consumer financial products and

---

[13]12 U.S.C. § 5512(c)(4). As defined by the Dodd-Frank Act, "covered persons" include any person that engages in offering or providing a consumer financial product or service and any affiliate of such a person if such affiliate acts as a service provider to such person. 12 U.S.C. § 5481(6). "Service providers" include any person that provides a material service to a covered person in connection with the offering or provision by such covered person of a consumer financial product or service, including a person that participates in designing, operating, or maintaining the consumer financial product or service; or processes transactions relating to the consumer financial product or service. 12 U.S.C. § 5481(26).).

[14]12 U.S.C. § 5512(c)(4)(C).

[15]Under § 1026 of the Dodd-Frank Act, CFPB may also require reports of insured depository institutions and insured credit unions with total assets of $10 billion or less as necessary to support CFPB's role in implementing federal consumer financial laws, to support examination activities, and to assess and detect risks to consumers and consumer financial markets.

[16]12 U.S.C. § 5514(e).

GAO-14-758 CFPB Data Collections

services.[17] Section 1024 does not contain any explicit restrictions on CFPB's ability to collect personally identifiable financial information.

- **Supervision of large institutions and affiliates.** Section 1025 of the Dodd-Frank Act provides CFPB with supervisory authority over insured depository institutions and credit unions with assets of more than $10 billion and their affiliates, including the authority to collect information from them for purposes of detecting and assessing associated risks to consumers and to markets for consumer financial products and services.[18] CFPB also has some supervisory authority under section 1025 over service providers of insured depository institutions and credit unions with over $10 billion in assets, as well as service providers to a substantial number of insured depository institutions or credit unions with $10 billion or less in assets.[19] Section 1025 does not contain any explicit restrictions on CFPB's ability to collect personally identifiable financial information.

The Dodd-Frank Act also contains additional restrictions on CFPB's ability to collect consumer financial data and includes requirements on how such data must be protected once they are collected. The act requires CFPB to take steps to ensure that certain information, including personal information, is not disclosed to the public when such information is protected by law.[20] In addition, CFPB must not obtain personally identifiable financial information about consumers from the financial records of covered persons or service providers, unless consumers provide written permission, or other legal provisions specifically permit or require such collections.[21]

---

[17]12 U.S.C. § 5514(b)(1).

[18]12 U.S.C. § 5515(a),(b).

[19]12 U.S.C. §§ 5515(d), 5516(e).

[20]Specifically, section 1022(c)(8) of the act states that in collecting information from any person, publicly releasing information held by CFPB, or requiring covered persons to publicly report information, CFPB shall take steps to ensure that proprietary, personal, or confidential consumer information that is protected from public disclosure under FOIA, the Privacy Act, or any other provision of law, is not made public under Title X of the Dodd-Frank Act. 12 U.S.C. § 5512(c)(8).

[21]12 U.S.C. § 5512(c)(9).

The Role of the Federal Prudential Regulators

CFPB interacts with other financial regulators that also collect consumer financial data and have responsibility for overseeing federal consumer financial laws. These agencies include the four prudential regulators that supervise depository institutions for safety and soundness of their financial condition:

- OCC charters and supervises national banks and federal thrifts;

- the Federal Reserve supervises state-chartered banks that opt to be members of the Federal Reserve System, bank holding companies, thrift holding companies, the nondepository institution subsidiaries of those institutions, and nonbanks designated as significantly important by the Financial Stability Oversight Council;

- FDIC supervises FDIC-insured state-chartered banks that are not members of the Federal Reserve System and federally insured state savings banks and thrifts; insures the deposits of all banks and thrifts approved for federal deposit insurance; and resolves by sale or liquidation all failed insured banks and thrifts and certain nonbank financial companies; and

- NCUA charters and supervises federally chartered credit unions and insures savings in federally and most state-chartered credit unions.

As part of their overall supervision programs, the prudential regulators have consumer compliance examination authority for insured depository institutions with $10 billion or less in assets and CFPB is required to coordinate its supervisory activities with the supervisory activities of the prudential regulators for insured depository institutions with more than $10 billion in assets.[22] Most of the depository institutions CFPB supervises for consumer protection are supervised for safety and soundness by OCC, the Federal Reserve, or FDIC and at a holding company level by the Federal Reserve. The Dodd-Frank Act requires CFPB to coordinate its supervisory actions and examinations of large depository institutions with the prudential regulators.

---

[22]Although the Dodd-Frank Act refers to depository institutions and credit unions separately, for the purposes of this report we are including credit unions in our description of depository institutions unless otherwise noted.

Other Requirements and Standards Related to Federal Data Collection Efforts

Various other federal requirements apply to CFPB and other federal agencies' data collection activities. The Paperwork Reduction Act (PRA) requires agencies to obtain OMB approval for identical collections of information from 10 or more individuals or entities.[23] For data collections meeting the criteria of the act, agencies must seek public comment in the *Federal Register* and consult with the public and affected agencies on ways to minimize the burden associated with information collections and other issues. The general purposes of PRA include minimizing the federal paperwork burden for individuals, small businesses, state and local governments, and other persons; minimizing the cost to the federal government of collecting, maintaining, using, and disseminating information; and maximizing the usefulness of information collected by the federal government. The Office of Information and Regulatory Affairs within OMB provides oversight over federal data collections and PRA compliance.

The Privacy Act of 1974 and the E-Government Act of 2002, which establish privacy and information security requirements for federal agencies, also govern CFPB's use of consumer financial data.[24] The Privacy Act places limitations on the collection, disclosure, and use of personal information maintained in "systems of records," or groups of records under the control of any agency from which information is retrieved by individual name or identifier.[25] For example, agencies must: (1) maintain in records only such information about an individual as is relevant and necessary to accomplish a purpose of the agency required by statute or executive order; (2) establish rules of conduct for persons involved in the design, development, operation, or maintenance of any system of records, or in maintaining any record, and instruct each such person with respect to those rules and the requirements of the act; and (3) establish appropriate administrative, technical, and physical

---

[23]Pub. L. No. 104-13, 109 Stat. 163 (1995) (codified as amended at 44 U.S.C. §§ 3501-3521). The approval applies whether the collections are mandatory or voluntary.

[24]Privacy Act of 1974, Pub. L. No. 93-579, 88 Stat. 1896 (1974) (codified as amended at 5 U.S.C. § 552a); E-Government Act of 2002, Pub. L. No. 107-347, 116 Stat. 2899 (2002).

[25]5 U.S.C. § 552a(a)(5). According to the Privacy Act, a "record" means any item, collection, or grouping of information about an individual that is maintained by an agency, including, but not limited to, his or her education, financial transactions, medical history, and criminal or employment history and that contains his or her name, or the identifying number, symbol, or other identifying particular assigned to the individual, such as a finger or voice print or a photograph. 5 U.S.C. § 552a(a)(4).

safeguards to ensure the security and confidentiality of records and to protect against any anticipated threats or hazards to their security or integrity that could result in substantial harm, embarrassment, inconvenience, or unfairness to any individual on whom information is maintained. The Privacy Act also requires agencies to notify the public in the *Federal Register* when they establish or make changes to a system of records. Among the things this notice must identify are: the categories of data collected; the categories of individuals about whom information is collected; the intended "routine" uses of data; and procedures that individuals can use to review and correct information about them.

The privacy provisions of the E-Government Act of 2002 require that agencies conduct privacy impact assessments before developing, using, or contracting for an information security system that contains personal information.[26] These assessments are analyses of how personal information is collected, stored, shared, and managed in a federal system. According to OMB guidance, the purpose of such assessments is to (1) ensure handling conforms to applicable legal, regulatory, and policy requirements regarding privacy; (2) determine the risks and effects of collecting, maintaining, and disseminating information in identifiable form in an electronic information system; and (3) examine and evaluate protections and alternative processes for handling information to mitigate potential privacy risks.

Title III of the E-Government Act, known as the Federal Information Security Management Act of 2002 (FISMA), established a framework designed to ensure the effectiveness of security controls of information and information systems that support federal operations and assets. This includes the information and information systems that are provided or managed by another agency, contractor, or other source (known as third-party providers). FISMA assigns specific responsibilities to the head of an agency to provide information security protections commensurate with the

---

[26]Pub. L. No. 107-347, § 208, 116 Stat. at 2921 (2002) (codified at 44 U.S.C. § 3501 note). The privacy provisions of the E-Government Act apply to "information in identifiable form," which OMB has defined as information in an information technology system or online collection (i) that directly identifies an individual (e.g., name, address, social security number or other identifying number or code, telephone number, email address, etc.) or (ii) by which an agency intends to identify specific individuals in conjunction with other data elements, i.e., indirect identification. See Office of Management and Budget, *OMB Guidance for Implementing the Privacy Provisions of the E-Government Act of 2002*, OMB Memorandum M-03-22 (Washington, D.C.: Sept. 26, 2003).

risk and magnitude of the harm resulting from unauthorized access, use, disclosure, disruption, modification, or destruction of information collected or maintained by or on behalf of the agency.

FISMA also states that agencies are to develop, document, and implement an agency-wide information security program. The information security program should include

- periodic assessments of the risk and magnitude of harm that could result from the unauthorized access, use, disclosure, disruption, modification, or destruction of information or information systems;

- policies and procedures that (1) are based on risk assessments, (2) cost-effectively reduce information security risks to an acceptable level, (3) ensure that information security is addressed throughout the life-cycle of each system, and (4) ensure compliance with applicable requirements;

- subordinate plans for providing adequate information security for networks, facilities, and systems or groups of information systems, as appropriate;

- security awareness training to inform personnel of information security risks and of their responsibilities in implementing agency policies and procedures, as well as training personnel with significant security responsibilities for information security;

- periodic testing and evaluation of the effectiveness of information security policies, procedures, and practices, to be performed with a frequency depending on risk, but no less than annually—including testing of management, operational, and technical controls for every system identified in the agency's required inventory of major information systems;

- a process for planning, implementing, evaluating, and documenting remedial action to address any deficiencies in the information security policies, procedures, and practices of the agency;

- procedures for detecting, reporting, and responding to security incidents; and

- plans and procedures to ensure continuity of operations for information systems that support the operations and assets of the agency.

To assist agencies in meeting the requirements of FISMA, NIST was tasked with developing standards and guidelines for agencies. NIST has issued a series of special publications addressing privacy and security concerns both at organizational and information system levels that federal agencies generally follow.

- **Security and Privacy Controls:** NIST Special Publication 800-53 gives agencies guidance on selecting and specifying security and privacy controls to meet federal standards and requirements.[27] According to NIST, the guidance provides a holistic approach to information security and risk management by providing organizations with the breadth and depth of security controls necessary to fundamentally strengthen their information systems and the environments in which those systems operate. The guidance also organizes privacy controls into eight areas: authority and purpose; accountability, audit, and risk management; data quality and integrity; data minimization and retention; individual participation and redress; security; transparency; and use limitation. These controls are based on the Fair Information Practice Principles, an internationally recognized privacy framework.[28]

- **Protecting Personal Information:** NIST Special Publication 800-122 provides guidelines for agencies to use in developing a risk-based approach for protecting personal information.[29] NIST recommends that agencies evaluate how easily information can be used to identify specific individuals and evaluate the sensitivity of each individual data field, as well as the sensitivity of the collective data fields.

---

[27]National Institute of Standards and Technology, *Security and Privacy Controls for Federal Information Systems and Organizations,* Special Publication (SP) 800-53, Revision 4 (Apr. 30, 2013).

[28]The Fair Information Practice Principles were first proposed in 1973 by a U.S. government advisory committee. They are used with some variation by agencies and organizations to address privacy considerations and are the basis of privacy laws and related policies in the United States and other countries. They are not legal requirements but a framework of principles for balancing the need for privacy with other public policy interests, such as national security, law enforcement, and administrative efficiency. See GAO, *Privacy: Alternatives Exist for Enhancing Protection of Personally Identifiable Information,* GAO-08-536 (Washington, D.C.: May 19, 2008).

[29]NIST, *Guide to Protecting the Confidentiality of Personally Identifiable Information (PII),* Special Publication (SP) 800-122 (Gaithersburg, Md.: April 2010).

- **Information Security Risk Management Framework:** NIST Special Publication 800-37 describes a security risk-management framework for use by federal agencies and their contractors.[30] This framework is a six-step process that helps agencies integrate information security and risk-management activities into the system development life-cycle.

CFPB's Privacy and Information Security Program

When CFPB began operations in 2011, it relied on the information security program and systems of the U.S. Department of the Treasury (Treasury). As the agency has grown, CFPB has begun transferring its information infrastructure (including e-mails, file shares, and data storage) to an independent hardware and systems environment owned by CFPB, but at the time of our review, some of CFPB's data were still being transmitted using Treasury systems and CFPB was still using Treasury to manage its workstations.

CFPB created a Data Intake Group consisting of CFPB staff from across the agency with expertise in legal, cybersecurity, and privacy issues. CFPB staff told us the group was formed in spring 2013 and has evolved into a standard business practice. The group regularly meets to discuss proposed data collections and to help ensure the agency takes all steps required under applicable law or guidance.[31] CFPB staff said the group provides a forum for staff in various parts of the agency to raise issues relevant to their areas of expertise. For example, staff with legal expertise are expected to ensure appropriate use of collection authorities and compliance with any legal restrictions for a proposed data collection and staff with PRA expertise ensure that the group considers whether PRA might apply to the collection and whether to consult with OMB. The group's collective decision to proceed with a data collection is summarized in an e-mail to the Chief Information Officer, who makes the final determination about the proposed collection. CFPB staff who are involved in coordinating the Data Intake Group have begun compiling

---

[30]NIST, *Guide for Applying the Risk Management Framework to Federal Information Systems*, Special Publication 800-37, Revision 1 (Gaithersburg, Md.: February 2010).

[31]Before the establishment of the Data Intake Group, CFPB staff said they used an ad hoc process that relied on either the procurement process or requests for information technology support and infrastructure to assess proposals for new data collections. The Data Intake Group does not review enforcement data or data collected as part of supervisory exams as part of its intake group.

information about each approved data collection, although this effort is still at an early stage.

CFPB Collects a Wide Range of Consumer Financial Data

From January 2012 to July 2014, CFPB undertook 12 large-scale data collection efforts. These collections spanned products including mortgages, student loans, and credit cards, and have been used for a variety of purposes, such as informing rulemaking and statutorily required studies. CFPB obtains data for five of these collections on an ongoing basis; data for the other collections were obtained only once. The types of information in each consumer financial data collection vary depending on the product type and nature of the inquiry, and may include some account-level data (such as account balance and amount of available credit), transaction-level information (such as the timing of deposits or withdrawals in checking accounts, or merchant names for some transactions), or disclosures of product policies and terms. Some collections represent a sample of accounts from one source while others represent all data from selected institutions. The data come from a variety of sources, including financial institutions, credit reporting agencies, data aggregators, and industry groups.[32] Table 1 provides more information on these consumer financial data collections.

Table 1: CFPB's Large-Scale Collections of Consumer Financial Data from January 2012 through July 1, 2014

Data collection	Data collected (purpose and type)	Source	Scope	Ongoing or one-time?
Arbitration case records	Purpose: to assess consumer arbitration filings for credit card, checking, and payday loan products Type: electronic consumer case records from January 2010 through early 2013	Voluntarily provided by American Arbitration Association	11,204 case records	One-time
Automobile sales	Purpose: to monitor car sales volumes and financing Type: vehicle transaction-level data from 46 state motor vehicle departments matched with consumer credit data	Procured from Experian	700,000 vehicles per month	Ongoing (monthly)
Consumer credit report information	Purpose: to analyze changes in consumer behavior as it relates to debt Type: consumer credit information from a nationally representative sample of consumers and associated co-signers and co-borrowers	Procured from Experian	10.7 million consumers, co-signers, and co-borrowers	Ongoing (monthly and quarterly)

[32]For one data collection, CFPB staff told us that they have a contractual relationship with a vendor to collect data from several large banks that issue credit cards and to ensure the data are matched to credit reporting data appended by a national credit reporting agency.

GAO-14-758 CFPB Data Collections

Data collection	Data collected (purpose and type)	Source	Scope	Ongoing or one-time?
Credit cards	Purpose: to identify risks in the credit card market Type: individual consumers' credit card account-level data, with linkages to credit reporting data	9 large financial institutions using a commercial data aggregator[a]	25 to 75 million total accounts	Ongoing (monthly)
Credit scores	Purpose: to analyze differences between credit scores provided to consumers and creditors Type: random samples of consumer credit reports and credit scores calculated on such reports	Voluntarily provided by three credit reporting agencies (Experian, Equifax, and TransUnion)	600,000 total consumer credit reports	One-time
Deposit advance products	Purpose: to describe features of typical deposit advance products Type: deposit account and transaction-level data, including deposit advance product usage. Institutions provided all data on a 5 percent sample of deposit advance users and a 1 percent sample of eligible non-users	Several depository institutions offering deposit advance products	100,000 to 500,000 total accounts	One-time
Mortgages	Purpose: to monitor the mortgage market effectively for emerging trends Type: loan-level data from large servicers for mortgages (includes historical data dating to 1989)	Procured from CoreLogic	29 million active loans; 173 million total loans	Ongoing (monthly)
Online payday loans	Purpose: to better understand payday loan usage patterns and behaviors Type: summaries of online payday loans from a sample of borrower files matched with consumer credit data[b]	Procured from Clarity Services	300,000 borrowers	One-time
Overdraft fees	Purpose: to measure overdraft usage and costs Type: account and transaction-level data based on random samples of less than 5 percent of consumer checking accounts per bank	9 large banks	2 million accounts and related transactions	One-time
Private-label mortgages[c]	Purpose: to monitor the mortgage market effectively for emerging trends Type: residential mortgage loan data on all accounts packaged into private label mortgage-backed securities (includes historical data dating to 1999)	Procured from Blackbox Logic	4 million active loans; 21.9 million total loans	Ongoing (monthly)
Private student loans	Purpose: to describe private student lending products and performance Type: loan-level data on all educational loan originations from 2005 to 2011	Voluntarily provided by 9 large financial institutions	5.5 million total loans	One-time
Storefront payday loans	Purpose: to describe payday loan products and consumers' use of them Type: borrower-level activity for all loans provided within a period of 12 or more months	From 5 to 9 payday lenders	15-40 million total loans	One-time

Source: GAO analysis of CFPB information. | GAO-14-758

Notes: This table reflects large-scale data collections from multiple entities collected under several legal authorities that will be described later in this report. Not reflected in this table are consumer financial data from individual entities that CFPB collects through its enforcement and consumer response activities. In addition to these collections, CFPB has collected information on remittance transfers using data obtained before 2012, and has collected loan-level data on reverse mortgages from publicly available sources.

[a]CFPB has access to credit card data from 16 additional credit card issuers through an information-sharing agreement with OCC that is discussed later in this report. When combined, these data contain information about 87 percent of outstanding credit card balances by volume as of March 2014.

[b]The collection also included data on borrowers who had similar borrowing records to those who had used online payday loans but had not taken out an online payday loan.

[c]Private-label mortgages are not those securitized by the government-sponsored enterprises or Ginnie Mae.

As noted in table 1, CFPB's credit card and online payday collections include data from account holders' credit reports. For each of these collections, CFPB requests that consumers' account-level credit card or loan information is matched with their credit reports from the credit reporting agency. The credit reporting agency sends the combined data, which does not identify individual consumers, to CFPB through the commercial data aggregator. Aside from these two data collections, CFPB staff told us that large-scale collections are not aggregated or combined into larger databases.

CFPB Uses Its Supervisory Authorities to Collect Most Consumer Financial Data	CFPB staff told us that most of CFPB's large-scale data collections were conducted under its supervisory authorities. These authorities require CFPB to periodically require reports and conduct examinations of entities they oversee to assess compliance with federal consumer financial laws, obtain information about those entities' activities, and detect and assess risks to consumers and markets for consumer financial products and services. CFPB staff noted that financial institution representatives generally requested that CFPB collect data under its supervisory authority to provide the institutions with greater confidentiality and legal protections. CFPB staff stated that data collected under CFPB's supervisory authorities are considered confidential and therefore not subject to disclosure under certain federal information transparency requirements, such as the Freedom of Information Act. CFPB has used its supervisory authorities to collect certain data on credit cards, storefront payday loans, deposit advance products, and overdraft fees. Information collected under these authorities sometimes includes personally identifiable financial information.

CFPB staff told us they need to collect and review consumer financial data at the institution level to effectively carry out their supervisory authorities. For example, they told us that they have used the data obtained on credit cards to identify risks and areas to be reviewed during examinations of financial institutions. According to CFPB staff, these analyses can identify changes at a particular institution, such as an increase in late fees charged or allow comparisons that identify divergences in practices across institutions and help CFPB determine where to allocate its supervisory resources.

CFPB staff also noted that certain large-scale data collections facilitate a supervisory approach based on determining the relative risk consumer financial products and services posed to consumers in the relevant product and market. CFPB staff noted that this supervisory approach differs from the approaches the prudential regulators have taken.[33] Moreover, CFPB legal staff said use of consumer financial data collected under the agency's supervisory authorities for certain additional purposes is allowed under the Dodd-Frank Act. Specifically, CFPB legal staff noted the act authorizes CFPB to use information gathered from various sources, including "examination reports concerning covered persons or service providers," to conduct its market monitoring.[34] They said they interpret this provision as permitting them to use information gathered as part of the supervisory process for other purposes, including market monitoring. For example, CFPB staff told us they needed data on various markets because within their first 18 months of operations they had to issue numerous rules including those relating to electronic transfers of consumers' funds to recipients abroad (remittances), the characteristics of mortgages that would qualify lenders for protection from borrower lawsuits (qualified mortgage requirements), and prohibitions on incentives to steer borrowers to particular mortgage loans. CFPB staff told us the collections were necessary to help them understand the functioning of those markets and consumers' experience with them. CFPB also had to obtain data on markets that were previously unregulated, such as payday lending, credit reporting, and private student lending.

In addition to these large-scale collections, CFPB staff collect some consumer financial data from individual entities through the examination process, also under the agency's supervisory authorities. CFPB staff told us that collecting consumer financial data during examinations is key to helping them carry out their mission to supervise markets. Such data

---

[33]The Dodd Frank Act requires this approach for CFPB's supervision of nondepository covered persons. 12 U.S.C. § 5514(b)(2). To ensure consistency, CFPB staff said that they use a risk-based approach to supervision of all market participants, including large banks, thrifts, credit unions, and their affiliates.

[34]12 U.S.C. § 5512(c)(4)(B)(i).

allow CFPB's examiners to better understand the institution under review and inform the decisions they make about what areas and activities to include in the scope of examinations. Staff told us they collect information throughout the supervisory examination process in order to assess risk to consumers from particular financial institutions and to monitor markets. For example, CFPB staff collect market and institution data from available sources (for example, during a baseline review of an institution, from commercial data vendors, or from their own research staff or other federal regulators) before collecting an institution's consumer account information or internal documents relating to compliance management, such as training materials and internal policies. They explained that CFPB collected and analyzed data during the scoping phase to inform its supervisory staff about an institution's activities and identify the risks the activities pose.

Our analysis suggests that the scope and extent of the consumer financial data CFPB collected during individual examinations has varied. For example:

- We reviewed information request letters CFPB sent to a payday lender, debt collector, and credit reporting agency. In one of these letters, CFPB asked for detailed information about certain accounts, such as all new accounts or all consumer disputes within a certain review period. The data requests included account numbers, consumer contact records, and consumer disputes and their resolutions.

- We reviewed 46 examinations CFPB completed in 2012 and 2013 for 10 depository institutions that previously had been subject to prudential oversight by the Federal Reserve, OCC, or FDIC. Slightly more than half (25 of 46) of the examinations included requests for consumer financial data. During those examinations that included requests for consumer financial data, examiners sought data for a sample of accounts, such as accounts with deposit advance products. In other cases, examiners sought access to all accounts or loan applications, as with several mortgage or private student loan application examinations. Some CFPB examiners sought consumer financial data to verify the accuracy of mortgage loan data these institutions had been reporting to prudential regulators, pursuant to the requirements of the Home Mortgage Disclosure Act (HMDA).[35]

Representatives of the nine institutions we interviewed that had been providing consumer financial data to CFPB and the other regulators told us that CFPB's examination-related requests were more extensive than the data requests from their prudential regulators. According to CFPB staff, some of the differences arise because CFPB needed to obtain more comprehensive information on institutions that might not have been subject to the same level of consumer protection oversight before passage of the Dodd-Frank Act or were conducting activities that had raised supervisory concerns. CFPB staff told us examiners generally request financial institutions' account- and transaction-level data to conduct various analyses and test for compliance with relevant federal consumer financial laws, and they instruct institutions to alert CFPB if their prudential regulators already have collected the requested data, so that they can coordinate efforts.

CFPB Also Has Used Its Market Monitoring Authority and Voluntary Requests to Collect Data

CFPB also has used its market monitoring authority, as well as voluntary data submissions, to collect data. Under the Dodd-Frank Act, CFPB is prohibited from obtaining information under its market monitoring authority from covered persons and service providers participating in consumer financial services markets for purposes of gathering or analyzing the personally identifiable financial information of consumers, and none of these collections appeared to include personally identifiable financial information.[36] Data collected under the CFPB's market monitoring authorities included automobile sales, consumer credit report information, mortgage loan performance, and online payday loans. CFPB purchased these collections from commercial data aggregators, and each collection was obtained either monthly or quarterly (except for data on online payday loans, a one-time purchase). Other financial regulators, banks, and other financial market participants use many of these same commercial databases (such as those covering credit report information and mortgages).

---

[35]Pub. L. No. 94-200, Tit. III, 89 Stat. 1124, 1125 (1975) (codified as amended at 12 U.S.C. §§ 2801-2810).

[36]12 U.S.C. § 5512(c)(4)(C). We discuss how CFPB takes steps to comply with this restriction later in this report.

CFPB staff also told us that several voluntary data collections have been instrumental for three statutorily required reports on consumer financial products and markets.[37] For these reports, CFPB asked companies or industry associations to provide information on consumer financial products and services through voluntary, one-time collections. These voluntary collections included information on arbitration case records, consumer reports and credit reports, and private student loan data (described in table 1). The private student loan data collection informed CFPB's analysis of the number of loan originations and their associated interest rates and allowed CFPB to determine any trends in lending in the private student loan market. CFPB found that the market for private student loans had increased from 2003 to 2007 and lender underwriting requirements loosened.[38] Similarly, analysis of consumer credit report data informed CFPB's report comparing consumer and creditor-purchased credit scores.[39] See appendix II for additional information on CFPB's use of consumer financial data in its reports.

Prudential Regulators Collect Similarly Large Amounts of Consumer Financial Data

Like CFPB, the prudential regulators (FDIC, Federal Reserve, OCC, and NCUA) collect consumer financial data associated with products offered by the financial institutions they regulate. Staff from these regulators told us that they undertake the collections as part of their supervisory responsibilities to analyze markets that affect the institutions they oversee. For example, FDIC, OCC, and the Federal Reserve all obtain mortgage data, including loan origination dates, outstanding balances, and payment status, from commercial data aggregators similar to the aggregators CFPB has used. The Federal Reserve collects mortgage application data submitted under HMDA on behalf of CFPB, OCC, FDIC, NCUA, and the Department of Housing and Urban Development and aggregates these data on behalf of the Federal Financial Institutions Examination Council.[40] Federal Reserve staff told us the Federal Reserve

---

[37]The three reports were mandated in Dodd Frank Act §§ 1028(a), 1077, and 1078.

[38]See Consumer Financial Protection Bureau, *Private Student Loans* (Washington, D.C.: Aug. 29, 2012).

[39]See Consumer Financial Protection Bureau, *Analysis of Differences between Consumer- and Creditor-Purchased Credit Scores* (Washington, D.C.: September 2012).

[40]The Federal Reserve collects HMDA data as a third-party data collection service on behalf of the Federal Financial Institutions Examination Council, which provides a forum for the development and dissemination of jointly prepared guidance and other information for the depository institution regulators.

also purchases credit reporting data from credit reporting agencies. Furthermore, the Federal Reserve and OCC have ongoing data collections of credit card accounts that they obtain from financial institutions they supervise (using the same commercial data aggregator as CFPB). FDIC and NCUA staff told us FDIC and NCUA collect consumer financial data in their roles as insurers for banks and credit unions through the resolution process.[41] Table 2 provides information about OCC's, FDIC's, and the Federal Reserve's consumer financial data collections.

Table 2: Large-Scale Collections of Consumer Financial Data, by OCC, FDIC, and the Federal Reserve, as of July 1, 2014

Regulator[a]	Data collection	Data collected (purpose and type)	Source	Scope	Ongoing or one-time?	Contains information that directly identifies individuals?
Office of the Comptroller of the Currency	Credit cards	Purpose: to address risks in the credit card market Type: individual consumers' credit card account-level data, with linkages to credit reporting data	16 large national banks using a commercial data aggregator[b]	521 million total accounts	Ongoing (monthly)	No
	Mortgages	Purpose: to address risks in the mortgage market and report on first-lien residential mortgage data Type: first-lien mortgage loan data and home equity loans, junior liens, lines of credit and address matching for home equity loans and first-lien mortgages on all accounts	61 financial institutions for first-lien data; 64 financial institutions for home equity loans using a commercial data aggregator	25.6 million first-lien mortgage loans; 8 million home equity loans	Ongoing (monthly)	Yes[c]
Federal Reserve	Credit cards	Purpose: to assess the capital adequacy of selected institutions and conduct market supervision Type: loan-level and portfolio data on all individual consumers' credit card accounts	17 large bank holding companies using a commercial data aggregator	496 million total accounts[d]	Ongoing (monthly)	No

[41]FDIC uses a resolution process to address losses from failed insured banks and thrifts by selling a failed institution's assets and liabilities to another institution, liquidating the institution, or establishing an interim bridge bank. NCUA has similar responsibilities for failed credit unions.

Regulator[a]	Data collection	Data collected (purpose and type)	Source	Scope	Ongoing or one-time?	Contains information that directly identifies individuals?
	Mortgages	Purpose: to assess the capital adequacy of selected institutions and conduct market supervision Type: loan-level data on first-lien mortgage, home equity loans and lines of credit, and address matching for home equity loans and first-lien mortgages on all accounts	27 large bank holding companies using an aggregator provide the first-lien and address matching data; 24 large bank holding companies provide home equity loan data using a commercial data aggregator	29 million first-lien mortgages; 9 million home equity loans[d]	Ongoing (monthly)	Yes[c]
	Private-label mortgages[e]	Purpose: to monitor the mortgage markets Type: loan-level data on Alt-A and subprime loan performance and loan characteristics	Procured from CoreLogic	3 million active loans; 19.8 million total loans	Ongoing (monthly)	No
	Mortgages	Purpose: to monitor the mortgage markets Type: loan-level data on performance and loan characteristics for residential mortgages serviced by 24 servicers	Procured from Black Knight Data and Analytics (formerly known as McDash)	24.4 million active loans; 61.7 million total loans	Ongoing (monthly)	No
	Credit reporting data[f]	Purpose: to review consumer credit behavior over time Type: panel data of all credit records associated with addresses for representative 5 percent sample of individuals	Procured from Equifax	40 million total consumer credit reports	Ongoing (quarterly)	No
	Survey of Consumer Finances	Purpose: to obtain detailed information on households' financial condition Type: random sample of balance sheets, pensions, income, and demographic characteristics of U.S. households	Collected by the National Opinion Research Center on behalf of the Federal Reserve	6,500 households	Ongoing (triennial)	No
Federal Deposit Insurance Corporation	Nonprime private-label mortgages and securities[e]	Purpose: to monitor the mortgage markets Type: loan-level data on Alt-A and subprime loan performance and loan characteristics	Procured from Corelogic	2.9 million active loans; 19.8 million total loans[g]	Ongoing (monthly)	No
	Mortgages	Purpose: to monitor the mortgage markets Type: loan-level data on performance and loan characteristics for residential mortgages serviced by 24 servicers	Procured from Black Knight Data and Analytics (formerly known as McDash)	24.5 million active loans; 61.7 million total loans[g]	Ongoing (monthly)	No

Sources: GAO analysis of OCC, Federal Reserve, and FDIC information. | GAO-14-758

Generally, the large-scale data collections by the prudential regulators do not contain information that directly identifies individuals. As noted in table 2, both the Federal Reserve and OCC collect address data as part of their mortgage collections to match first-lien mortgages to home equity loans and lines of credit on the same property, but do not identify individual borrowers by name. Several of the regulators told us that they routinely collect consumers' personal information as part of their examinations of supervised entities but do not retain the information after the examination is completed. However, OCC told us that they generally only collect anonymized data from banks during examinations.

The Federal Reserve, OCC, and FDIC staff told us that they use these collections for research on consumer markets affecting the financial institutions they supervise. For example, OCC began its credit card collection in 2009 and it analyzes these data to better understand the credit card market in which large national banks operate, determine the current status of banks' credit card portfolios, and develop examination strategies. Like CFPB, OCC has contracted to have credit reporting agency attributes (such as the account holders' number of other accounts, outstanding balances, and their payment status) appended to the credit card account data supplied by banks. OCC uses the mortgage data it collects to develop its quarterly public Mortgage Metrics report and to further analyze trends in the mortgage marketplace.[42] The Federal Reserve relies on its credit card and mortgage data collections—part of institutions' broader data submissions—to support its assessments of the capital adequacy of bank holding companies (stress testing) and to more effectively supervise large banks.[43] Staff told us the Federal Reserve Bank of New York collects data on consumer credit reports to review anonymized consumers' credit behavior over time and they have published several reports on these data.[44] Federal Reserve staff and other researchers have used data from the Survey of Consumer Finances to issue numerous reports on trends in household wealth changes in the U.S.[45] FDIC staff told us they use the mortgage data the agency purchases to conduct market and aggregate-level research and analysis.

Other Federal Regulators Collect Consumer Data According to their Missions

We also examined the data collections of four other federal agencies with consumer protection responsibilities and found their collections generally were less extensive than CFPB's data collections. For example, SEC, which regulates the securities industry, and CFTC, which regulates the derivatives markets, collect only limited consumer financial data related to their roles in overseeing their respective industries. SEC staff told us the agency's mission generally does not necessitate large collections of consumer financial data, but that staff obtain some consumer financial

---

[42]For example, see Office of the Comptroller of the Currency, *OCC Mortgage Metrics Report: Disclosure of National Bank and Federal Savings Association Mortgage Loan Data, First Quarter 2014* (Washington, D.C.: June 2014). OCC began issuing these reports in 2008 and the reports include key performance data on first residential mortgages serviced by national banks, focusing on delinquencies, loss mitigation actions, and foreclosures.

[43]Financial institutions submit credit card and mortgage data to the Federal Reserve under what are called the Y-14 schedules. The data submissions are part of a larger data collection (including capital, assets, and liabilities) that the Federal Reserve uses to assess risks to the entities themselves and for mitigating risks to the financial stability of the United States (a process known as stress testing).

[44]For example, see Federal Reserve Bank of New York, *Quarterly Report on Household Debt and Credit, August 2014* (New York, NY: August 2014) and Federal Reserve Bank of New York, *Quarterly Report on Household Debt and Credit, May 2014* (New York, NY: May 2014).

[45]For example, see Board of Governors of the Federal Reserve System, *What's the Chance? Interviewers' Expectation of Response in the 2010 SCF,* (Washington, D.C.: September 2012) and Board of Governors of the Federal Reserve System, *Ponds and Streams: Wealth and Income in the U.S., 1989 to 2007,* (Washington, D.C.: January 2009).

data as part of their efforts to oversee the entities the agency regulates and to enforce the federal securities laws. CFTC staff similarly told us their agency is not required to undertake any large consumer financial data collections, but does obtain limited amounts of such information when reviewing traders and auditing futures market participants.

FTC, which is responsible for ensuring that consumers are protected from unfair or deceptive acts or practices, collects consumer complaint data to detect patterns of fraud and abuse. FTC compiles the data into a nonpublic database that is shared with other law enforcement agencies. Apart from this database, FTC staff told us that they review the complaints and other investigative information and generally do not compile other consumer information databases to detect fraud and deception. Staff from another agency that addresses consumer issues, the Consumer Product Safety Commission, also told us that their agency is not mandated to make any consumer data collections, but that they are required to maintain a public database containing complaints about consumer products that helps them promote the safety of consumer products. This agency also collects information relating to the causes and prevention of death, injury, and illness associated with consumer products.

CFPB and Other Regulators Have Established Information-Sharing Agreements, but Some Overlap Exists

CFPB's Information-Sharing Agreements and Coordination

To minimize overlap and burden on financial institutions, CFPB has coordinated with the prudential regulators and shared consumer financial data through various formal agreements. The Dodd-Frank Act mandates that CFPB coordinate with the prudential regulators on its supervisory examinations of large banks and credit unions.[46] CFPB supervisory staff told us that they interpret this mandate to include the sharing of information (which may include consumer financial data) collected during

---

[46]12 U.S.C. § 5515(b)(2), (e).

the examination process. As a result, CFPB has established a supervisory examination coordination framework that includes an overarching memorandum of understanding (MOU) on supervisory coordination with all the other prudential regulators for the sharing of supervisory information on an ongoing basis.[47]

In addition to the overarching MOU, CFPB also established three general information-sharing agreements with the prudential regulators—one with OCC, one with FDIC, and one with NCUA—which established how CFPB and these other agencies will share information in response to the transfer of consumer protection functions to CFPB as part of Title X of the Dodd-Frank Act.[48] The agreements describe what information the agencies agree to share, how the data would be shared, the security provisions required to protect the data, and processes for requesting data or sharing data with additional parties. These MOUs do not specify any sharing of large-scale collections of consumer financial data. OCC staff said that these general MOUs had been used to share examination reports and supervisory letters but had not been used to share consumer financial data. Federal Reserve staff told us that they would prepare separate MOUs to govern arrangements to share specific datasets with other agencies. As of July 2014, CFPB and the Federal Reserve did not

---

[47]In May 2012, CFPB and the prudential regulators entered into the supervisory coordination MOU to facilitate their compliance with the Dodd-Frank Act's coordination requirements. Consumer Financial Protection Bureau, *Memorandum of Understanding on Supervisory Coordination,* accessed on July 16, 2014. We discussed CFPB's MOUs with other regulators in GAO, *Dodd-Frank Regulations: Agencies Conducted Regulatory Analyses and Coordinated but Could Benefit from Additional Guidance on Major Rules,* GAO-14-67 (Washington, D.C.: Dec. 11, 2013).

[48]12 U.S.C. § 5581 (transferring certain consumer financial protection functions to CFPB). The Federal Reserve and Treasury had an MOU related to sharing information during the establishment of CFPB; CFPB staff told us that they are working on developing a separate information-sharing agreement with the Federal Reserve. NCUA, in addition to its information-sharing agreement with CFPB, also has an MOU for sharing consumer complaints with CFPB. In addition, CFPB has nine MOUs with seven separate federal agencies, including the U.S. Department of Justice and the U.S. Department of Housing and Urban Development. In some cases, the MOUs set up information-sharing arrangements and discuss coordination on efforts such as enforcement activities. We reviewed 26 MOUs CFPB has established with various state attorneys general, state banking regulators, two cities, and one American Indian tribe and found that they generally discussed information sharing and confidentiality and only one included a data-sharing arrangement for CFPB to receive consumer financial data from a state regulatory agency. We also reviewed three MOUs CFPB established with three private companies that allow CFPB to receive consumer financial data related to the manufactured housing loans industry and the payday lending industry.

have an information-sharing agreement related to the sharing of large-scale collections of consumer financial data.

CFPB has two information-sharing agreements relating to large-scale data collections—one current collection and one collection that was in development at the time of our review. In 2013, CFPB entered into an agreement with OCC covering any sharing of information from their respective credit card collections.[49] As a result of this agreement, CFPB accesses account-level data from the 16 institutions from which OCC collects data in addition to the 9 institutions from which CFPB collects data. In total, the collections cover approximately 87 percent of outstanding credit card balances by volume. The agreement establishes ownership of the data and how OCC and CFPB will coordinate on the collection of credit card data, including which data fields to collect, what validation checks should be done to verify the data, the timing of the collections, and how the agencies should communicate.

CFPB also established an interagency agreement with FHFA related to the development of the National Mortgage Database, which staff told us will provide a comprehensive view of the mortgage market and allow for greater mortgage market monitoring, supervision, and research.[50] FHFA has reported that it is developing the database partly to facilitate mandatory reporting requirements under the Housing and Economic Recovery Act of 2008.[51] CFPB staff told us that they do not plan to provide any nonpublic data to the database, and FHFA and CFPB staff said that neither agency will directly collect the primary information for the database. Rather, staff said the agencies will purchase the data from a credit reporting agency. The credit reporting agency will provide an anonymized 5 percent sample—which will include about 3.5 million currently active mortgages—of first-lien, single-family mortgage loans

---

[49]As mentioned previously, CFPB collects data from 9 large financial institutions that are different than the 16 from which OCC collects its credit card data. OCC staff told us that as of July 2014, they had not accessed any of the credit card data that CFPB collects.

[50]CFPB and FHFA have an interagency agreement for the National Mortgage Database that outlines the funding arrangement and resource commitments of both agencies, as well as rights to access the data. CFPB and FHFA staff told us that CFPB provides FHFA with funding and resources for the development of the National Mortgage Database in return for access to the data.

[51]Housing and Economic Recovery Act of 2008, Pub. L. No. 110-289, 122 Stat. 2654 (2008).

GAO-14-758 CFPB Data Collections

active as of 1998 or later that are reported to the credit reporting agency, as well as credit report information on the borrowers in the selected sample.[52] FHFA staff told us they approached CFPB to collaborate on the database because they felt that CFPB would be interested in the mortgage data and they did not want to duplicate efforts. CFPB has been funding half of the costs associated with database development, but CFPB staff told us that their involvement as of July 2014 in the development of the database has been limited.[53]

Representatives from most of the financial institutions we interviewed said they observed CFPB coordinating with other prudential regulators during examinations at their institutions, with a few noting that coordination between the regulators had been increasing. However, others noted areas where CFPB could improve coordination. For example, the Federal Reserve's Office of Inspector General, which conducts internal audits of CFPB's operations, noted in a recent report that (1) CFPB did not consistently retain evidence of its information-sharing activities with prudential regulators and (2) CFPB could take additional steps to improve coordination with the prudential regulators by sharing draft supervisory letters (which describe the scope and findings of the examinations and highlight any corrective actions that should be taken) as part of these interactions.[54] In addition, a 2013 report issued by the Bipartisan Policy Center, which studies federal regulatory issues, found that CFPB's examination efforts focus more on the products that institutions offer rather than the examination efforts of the prudential regulators. The center's report notes that the difference in approach means it can take

---

[52]The National Mortgage Database will contain mortgage performance information as well as performance on other credit lines held by the mortgage's borrowers collected directly from the credit reporting agency. Additional information on the sample mortgages will be drawn from administrative files obtained from Fannie Mae and Freddie Mac. In addition, FHFA staff said they hope to merge mortgage data from the Federal Housing Administration, the Department of Veterans Affairs, and other sources.

[53]CFPB staff told us that although they are involved in the National Mortgage Database development through staff and financial support, they have deferred most of the administrative and development decisions to FHFA. FHFA's data servers will house the database and CFPB will have a limited number of staff with access. We did not include the National Mortgage Database in our larger review of CFPB databases because it is in development and the scope was not fully defined at the time of our review.

[54]See Board of Governors of the Federal Reserve System, Consumer Financial Protection Bureau, Office of Inspector General, *CFPB Can Improve the Efficiency and Effectiveness of Its Supervisory Activities*, 2014-AE-C-005 (Washington, D.C.: Mar. 27, 2014).

CFPB longer to complete its examinations and can make coordination between the regulators more challenging. The center recommended that CFPB and the prudential regulators coordinate more closely to better integrate CFPB's product-based approach and examination schedule with the other regulators' approach.

Some Overlap Exists in CFPB, OCC, and Federal Reserve Data Collections

Although CFPB, OCC, and the Federal Reserve often collect different information from different financial institutions, our analysis found some similarities in the types of data collected and overlap in the financial institutions reporting to each regulator in their large-scale mortgage and credit card collections (submitted directly from the institutions themselves).[55] The extent to which the same institutions provided the same types of data to CFPB, OCC, and the Federal Reserve is shown in figure 1 below.[56]

---

[55]Although all the regulators collect mortgage data, as of July 2, 2014, CFPB was not collecting any mortgage data directly from financial institutions or covered entities on an ongoing basis.

[56]We plan to examine issues related to fragmentation, overlap, and duplication in more depth in our ongoing work examining the current financial regulatory structure, which we anticipate issuing in 2015.

Figure 1: Similarities and Overlap in Financial Institutions and Data Fields Reporting Consumer Financial Data to CFPB, OCC, and the Federal Reserve, as of July 2014

Number of institutions

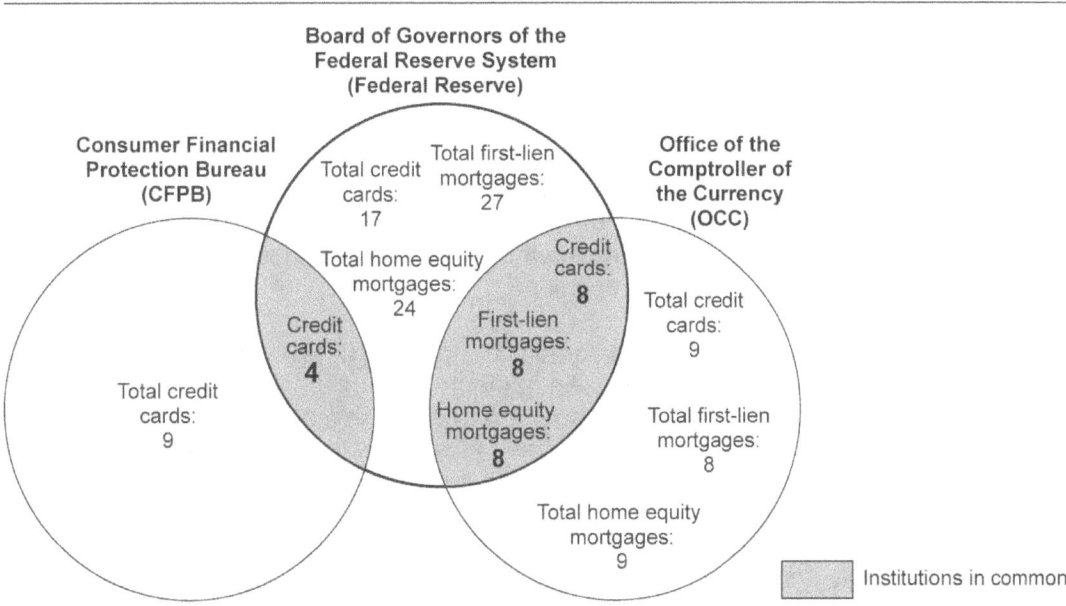

Number of data fields

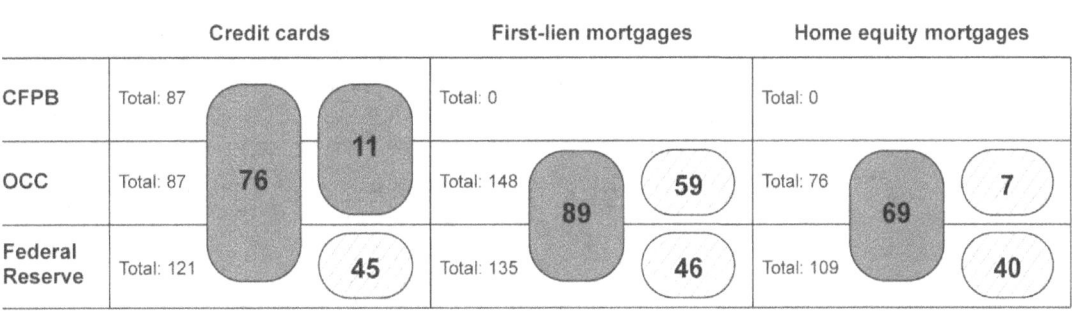

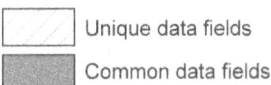 Unique data fields

Common data fields

Source: GAO analysis of data from CFPB, OCC, and Federal Reserve. | GAO-14-758

Note: CFPB and OCC collect the same data fields in their respective credit card collections, but from different financial institutions. For the OCC and Federal Reserve collections, one institution refers to one bank holding company submitting data to the Federal Reserve, but in some instances multiple national banks within those holding companies submit data to OCC.

As shown in figure 1, CFPB and OCC collect similar credit card information, but from different institutions.[57] However, as figure 1 also shows, four institutions that provide credit card data to CFPB also currently provide the same types of data to the Federal Reserve. However, staff from the two regulators noted that each uses its data for different purposes. As mentioned earlier, CFPB staff told us that they use the data obtained from their credit card collection to better understand card markets and help ensure compliance with federal consumer financial protection laws through the supervision and examination process. In contrast, the Federal Reserve uses the information in analyses that assess how changes in market conditions could affect the credit card accounts in ways that impact the safety and soundness of these institutions' holding companies.

Our analysis also found some overlap in the data collections of OCC and the Federal Reserve. Fifteen of the 16 national banks submitting credit card data to OCC submit similar data through eight holding companies to the Federal Reserve. In addition, 48 national bank affiliates that report mortgage data to OCC also report these data through their eight holding companies to the Federal Reserve. As a result, the holding company-level data the Federal Reserve obtains provides it with the information on these activities conducted by any national bank affiliates and non-national bank affiliates as well. OCC staff noted that OCC began its collection of mortgage data in March 2008 and credit card data in April 2009 in response to market events at the time. The Federal Reserve first proposed collecting similar credit card and mortgage data in February 2012. Subsequently, in a notice published in the *Federal Register* in June 2012, the Federal Reserve noted that its own collection effort was necessary because it needed data at the holding company level for its stress test analyses of the institutions, whereas OCC's data collection was only from the institutions' national bank affiliates.[58] Federal Reserve staff told us that the purpose of their collection is to assess the impact of economic changes on credit card accounts and how this affects the

---

[57]As of July 2014, regulatory staff told us CFPB accesses credit card data collected by OCC, but OCC does not access data collected by CFPB.

[58]See 77 Fed. Reg. 32,970 (June 4, 2012). OCC and Federal Reserve staff told us they share the credit card data they collect for those institutions over which they have joint supervision. The Federal Reserve's mortgage and credit card collections are part of a larger collection of data from bank holding companies (including company earnings, equity, and credit risk) that the Federal Reserve uses to meet requirements under the Dodd-Frank Act.

soundness of the holding companies, whereas OCC staff told us that they use the credit card data they collect to monitor the status of the national banks' credit card portfolios and identify potential issues to review in examinations. Staff from the Federal Reserve and OCC said they coordinated on development of their respective collections, aligned data fields, and established an information-sharing agreement to share account-level data for the institutions. However, OCC staff told us that coordinating the collections has been challenging and that one regulator can make changes to its respective collection without the consent of the other regulator.

Limited Information Exists on the Costs of CFPB's Data Collections and Views about the Benefits Varied

Limited quantitative information about costs of CFPB's large-scale data collections is available. CFPB's consumer financial data collections were not conducted through a rulemaking and therefore CFPB was not required to conduct a formal cost-benefit analysis before undertaking the collections.[59] But CFPB has identified some of the costs its data collections pose. After obtaining CFPB contracts relating to data acquisition, we determined that since 2011 CFPB has entered into five contracts with private firms to obtain consumer financial data. These contracts cover as long as 5 years, with obligations totaling over $33 million over this span, although CFPB staff noted that they would not expend this entire amount if some option years are not exercised.[60] CFPB staff reported that they were unable to quantify other costs borne by the agency, such as those relating to storing the data collected.

CFPB staff acknowledged that their collections create costs and some burden for financial institutions, but also noted the primary benefit of these collections is that they provide data that inform much of CFPB's work to protect consumers, including its supervisory process, rulemakings, and reports. For example, staff told us that the analysis from

---

[59]CFPB must conduct cost benefit analysis in prescribing rules under the federal consumer financial laws. See 12 U.S.C. 5512(b)(2). The data collections described earlier were not conducted through a rulemaking, and as such CFPB did not conduct a formal cost-benefit analysis.

[60]In responses to written questions for a congressional hearing, CFPB reported that the cost to date of its contracts to obtain data were just over $13 million for fiscal years 2012 and 2013. CFPB reported that both fiscal years include contracts with commercial and government vendors. See Subcommittee on Financial Institutions and Consumer Credit, House Committee on Financial Services, *Examining How the Consumer Financial Protection Bureau Collects and Uses Consumer Data*, 113th Cong., 1st sess. (July 9, 2013).

their ongoing credit card collections will provide input into the scope of some of CFPB's 2015 supervisory examinations of credit card issuers and will continue to help determine the scope of the agency's examinations. Staff also said that they used data from the credit card collection to inform part of CFPB's "ability to repay" rule, which amended requirements so that card issuers no longer had to consider whether certain younger consumers have an independent ability to pay; the previous rule had affected the ability of nonworking spouses or partners of these consumers to obtain credit.[61]

Some of the consumer and industry groups we interviewed agreed that CFPB collections of consumer financial data produced benefits and said CFPB needed this type of data to carry out its mission. For example, one group explained that the data are needed to aid CFPB staff's understanding of the financial products CFPB regulates. Two other groups said that CFPB's data collections may be justified because the collections help CFPB regulate and monitor the markets. In addition, one of the two groups said that CFPB's collections result in more informed decisions and actions, such as more targeted regulations. Furthermore, representatives from several privacy groups and one consumer group we interviewed noted that the commercial aggregators are more likely to be targeted by individuals seeking unauthorized access to consumer information than would CFPB.

However, representatives of financial institutions we interviewed had differing perspectives on the relative costs and benefits of providing data to CFPB. Representatives of most of the financial institutions we interviewed said that CFPB requests for consumer financial data during supervisory examinations have been more extensive than those of their prudential regulators. They said CFPB's data requests were broader and required more information than requests from their prudential regulators. However, some representatives offered explanations for these differences, noting that CFPB's focus for its collections (consumer protection) is different from the focus of their prudential regulators and CFPB's examiners must collect more data to familiarize themselves with the institutions they oversee.

---

[61]Truth in Lending (Regulation Z), 78 Fed. Reg. 35,818 (May 3, 2013).

Representatives of five institutions providing credit card data to CFPB's ongoing credit card collection generally reported that the initial submission process was burdensome, but costs to supply the data decreased over time. Representatives from several institutions reported that determining what data to submit to CFPB and how to provide them was particularly burdensome. For example, representatives cited challenges in consolidating different data on their credit card accounts from across different areas within their financial institutions and in establishing new internal procedures for reviewing the monthly data submission. However, the majority of financial institution representatives we interviewed stated that costs or the amount of time their staff spend preparing these data submissions has decreased over time.

In contrast, representatives of some financial industry and business trade associations we interviewed expressed concerns about the burden CFPB data collections place on financial institutions. Several representatives cited the costs to produce consumer financial data for CFPB, suggesting it may be greater than collections for other regulators. The recent report by the Bipartisan Policy Center noted that the impact of CFPB's data requests create real costs for entities because of the size of requests and institutions can be affected differently depending on their size.[62]

Other groups reported industry concerns about reputational risks they might face if the consumer financial data they submitted were inadvertently disclosed. For example, in a letter to CFPB, the U.S. Chamber of Commerce cited the potential for consumers to file litigation against the financial institutions that provided data to CFPB in the event that CFPB could not maintain the confidentiality of data collected from those entities.[63] CFPB staff noted that it would be difficult to determine liabilities in the event of a data breach without assuming certain details on the extent of breach and its cause. They said that in the event of a breach or unauthorized disclosure of data CFPB collected (including data a third-party collected on its behalf), affected consumers would receive credit monitoring or be provided relief similar to relief that other government

---

[62]Bipartisan Policy Center, *The Consumer Financial Protection Bureau: Measuring the Progress of a New Agency*, (Washington, D.C.: September 2013).

[63]Letter of David Hirschmann, Senior Vice President, U.S. Chamber of Commerce, to CFPB Director Richard Cordray, June 19, 2013.

GAO-14-758 CFPB Data Collections

agencies have provided, which other federal agencies or private organizations that experienced breaches have done.

CFPB has taken steps to minimize burden on financial institutions. For example, instead of requesting that the same institutions provide CFPB with credit card data, CFPB entered into a MOU with OCC to share the credit card data they collect. CFPB staff also reported coordinating their examination information requests with the other prudential regulators. CFPB staff said that they try to inform other regulators 90 days before sending information requests so that they can coordinate information requests when possible. In its information request letters, CFPB instructs institutions to alert CFPB if the institutions' prudential regulator already obtained the information CFPB requested. CFPB then would coordinate its requests with the regulator and alleviate the burden on the institution.

In a letter to the House Financial Services Committee, an economist noted that CFPB could obtain a 1 percent sample of credit card accounts to achieve its goals and also reduce some of the concerns relating to the costs of providing an entire portfolio of data.[64] We agree that providing samples of data, as opposed to entire portfolios of data, sometimes can reduce the burden on financial institutions. However, the regulators and institutions we interviewed and our analysis indicated obtaining only samples could hamper CFPB's regulatory efforts and likely would not produce cost savings for institutions.

CFPB uses samples in some examinations, but agency staff told us that they collect all accounts for the ongoing credit card collection—because the effort required to maintain a sample that represents the population of accounts would be burdensome to institutions. For example, if too many accounts in that sample are closed or the sample did not include newly created accounts, it would become less representative over time. Rather than having the institution re-sample its credit card population for each data submission, CFPB asks for all accounts on file. Similarly, OCC staff said that collecting samples of data on an ongoing basis would be less cost effective because they would have to redesign the sample for the institutions each time they wanted to conduct a different analysis. They said the additional requests for different samples would create further

---

[64]Letter to Representative Scott Garrett from Thomas Stratmann, George Mason University, dated January 23, 2014.

burden on the financial institutions.[65] In addition, representatives from nearly all the financial institutions with whom we spoke said that supplying CFPB with a sample of credit card data rather than all accounts would not significantly reduce submission costs. They explained that providing a sample might reduce data storage costs, but the submission process would remain the same. GAO staff with expertise in research methodologies and statistics reviewed information related to CFPB's credit card collection and agreed that that obtaining all accounts rather than a sample is likely more efficient for creating and maintaining a dataset that tracks changes in the same accounts over time. For example, over time, cardholders may close some accounts, which would create the burden and costs of continually adjusting the sample by adding other accounts to maintain the desired level of precision in the sample.

CFPB Lacks Written Procedures and Documentation Needed to Address Privacy Risks and Better Ensure Ongoing Compliance with Requirements

CFPB has taken steps to protect the privacy of consumers and comply with requirements, restrictions, and recommended practices in the Dodd-Frank Act, PRA, Privacy Act, E-Government Act, and NIST guidelines. These steps include creating privacy policies, issuing public notices of data collection activities, and establishing a group to consider and assure the appropriateness of proposed data collections. However, CFPB has not yet developed and implemented written procedures for its data intake process, which includes a review of proposed data collections for compliance with specific Dodd-Frank restrictions (among other things) and for anonymizing data. The agency also does not have written procedures for obtaining and documenting PRA determinations. CFPB and OCC have an information-sharing agreement for their respective credit card collections, but OMB staff raised concerns that such an agreement may require OMB review and approval. In addition, OCC has not obtained OMB approval for its credit card and mortgage data collections under PRA. Finally, CFPB generally met statutory privacy requirements, but lacked elements of certain privacy controls.

---

[65]We previously reported on the challenges regulators faced when not using a large enough population of mortgage files. For example, if the Federal Reserve had used a larger sample size for its initial review of mortgage files, the review process might have been more timely and identified harmed borrowers more quickly. See GAO, *Foreclosure Review: Lessons Learned Could Enhance Continuing Reviews and Activities under Amended Consent Orders*, GAO-13-277 (Washington, D.C.: Mar. 26, 2013).

CFPB Lacks Written Procedures for Data Intake

CFPB reviews data collections to determine whether the Dodd-Frank Act's restrictions apply, but it has not yet created written procedures for its data intake process.

Dodd-Frank Restrictions and Applicability to Data Collections

Under the act, CFPB must not obtain personally identifiable financial information about consumers from the records of covered persons or service providers, unless (a) consumers provide written permission or (b) other legal provisions specifically permit or require such collections.[66] However, CFPB legal staff cited the agency's supervisory authorities as being among the legal provisions that permit collections of consumers' personally identifiable financial information.[67] In particular, these staff said that CFPB's supervisory authorities permit the agency to compel entities it oversees to provide information (which, according to CFPB staff, may include consumers' personally identifiable financial information) it needs to assess compliance with federal consumer laws and detect and assess risks to consumers and markets. Therefore, information obtained through supervisory activities, such as information requested during examinations of large depository and certain nondepository institutions, does not violate the restriction on collection of personally identifiable financial information without consumer permission or as permitted by law, according to CFPB's legal staff. As mentioned earlier, the act has an additional restriction that prohibits CFPB from using its market monitoring authority, which enables CFPB to gather data to monitor risks to consumers to support its rulemaking and other functions, to obtain records from covered persons and service providers participating in consumer financial services markets for the purposes of gathering or analyzing the personally identifiable financial information of consumers.[68] CFPB defines "personally identifiable financial information" by regulation and states that data that do not contain direct personal identifiers such as account numbers, names,

---

[66]12 U.S.C. § 5512(c)(9).

[67]According to CFPB legal staff, CFPB's supervisory authorities in 12 U.S.C. §§ 5514-5515 trigger the exception in 12 U.S.C. § 5512(c)(9)(ii), which states that CFPB can collect personally identifiable financial information of consumers from covered persons when specifically permitted or required by other applicable laws, consistent with the exception granted to CFPB in the Right to Financial Privacy Act, as amended by the Dodd-Frank Act. 12 U.S.C. § 3413(r).

[68]12 U.S.C. § 5512(c)(4)(C).

or addresses do not meet the definition of "personally identifiable financial information."[69]

As shown in table 3, most of the data collections CFPB obtained do not directly identify individuals and therefore, according to CFPB staff, their contents do not meet the definition of "personally identifiable financial information." We analyzed the data fields and field descriptions for CFPB's 12 consumer financial data collections in our review and found that 9 collections do not include direct personal identifiers among the fields of information CFPB obtained. To the extent that the providers of the data (e.g., financial institutions and credit reporting agencies) had direct personal identifiers in their internal systems related to the nine collections, they did not include them in the data they provided to CFPB. We also visually inspected data extracts for 4 of these 9 data collections—credit cards, consumer credit report information, overdraft fees, and private student loans—and further verified that the data in the fields CFPB obtained did not directly identify individuals.

Table 3: Existence of Personal Identifiers in CFPB's Data Collections, as of July 2014

Data collection	Contains information that directly identifies individuals?	Collected from covered persons or service providers?	Collected under market monitoring authority?
Arbitration case records	✓		✓
Automobile sales			✓
Consumer credit report information			✓
Credit cards		✓	
Credit scores			✓
Deposit advance products	✓	✓	
Mortgages			✓
Private-label mortgages			✓
Online payday loans			✓
Overdraft fees		✓	
Private student loans		✓	✓
Storefront payday loans	✓	✓	

Source: GAO analysis of CFPB information. | GAO-14-758

[69]12 C.F.R. § 1016.3(q)(2).

Three of the data collections directly identified individuals using names and addresses. CFPB staff said that the Dodd-Frank restrictions did not apply to one of the three collections—arbitration case records—because the entity that voluntarily provided the data was not a covered person or service provider from which CFPB was prohibited from obtaining personally identifiable financial information. According to CFPB staff, the other two data collections that included direct personal identifiers—deposit advance products and storefront payday loans— were obtained from covered persons but do not violate Dodd-Frank restrictions because they were collected under CFPB's supervisory authority and not its market monitoring authority.

CFPB Actions to Anonymize Data

CFPB has taken steps, such as adopting informal procedures for anonymizing data, to remove the information that directly identifies consumers from these collections before the data are made available to staff for analysis that may have nonsupervisory purposes. In particular:

- **Deposit advance products:** CFPB staff showed us that for deposit advance products, each institution had provided the consumers' personal data—including names and addresses—in a file separate from files containing the account and transaction data. CFPB staff who analyze these data had not been granted access to these files. We reviewed files from two of the institutions that submitted data and confirmed that consumers were not directly identified in the files available to staff who work on large-scale data collections.

- **Storefront payday loans:** A CFPB staff member made copies of the files sent by the payday lenders and removed all the directly identifying information—names and complete address information. We observed files from three of the lenders that submitted data and confirmed that consumers were not directly identified in the files available to staff who analyze these data. The original files were stored in a separate file directory with restricted access, and CFPB staff who analyze these data did not have access.

CFPB staff also applied similar procedures to the overdraft fees data collection. This collection did not contain fields that directly identified consumers but had information—nine-digit zip codes (five-digit zip code plus the four-digit geographic extension)—that CFPB staff said they considered sensitive. CFPB staff replaced the zip codes with a randomly generated number string to further anonymize individuals. Staff stored the files with the original zip codes and the match key to the random strings that had replaced the zip codes in a separate location from the analysis files. We reviewed files from two of the institutions that submitted data and confirmed that consumers were not directly identified in the files available to staff who analyze these data.

For initial determinations of whether Dodd-Frank restrictions apply to a particular data collection, CFPB staff stated they rely on the legal division to raise any concerns during Data Intake Group meetings when proposals for data collections are considered. Legal staff said that their reviews consist of determining whether the data will be collected from a covered person or service provider, whether the collection will include personally identifiable financial information, and whether CFPB plans to anonymize a collection that contains personally identifiable financial information. Under current practice, legal staff participating in the Data Intake Group complete a section of a worksheet to indicate under what authority CFPB is obtaining the data and the type of agreement (such as a contract or interagency agreement) by which it would obtain the data. The legal division must review and vote to proceed on every proposed data collection before data may be brought into or collected by CFPB. However, CFPB staff told us the Data Intake Group as a whole does not have written procedures to guide its reviews. They said they recognized the lack of written procedures and documentation requirements for the Data Intake Group was a weakness in their current practices. CFPB's Chief Information Officer told us that CFPB established a data governance working group to formalize CFPB's information governance policies, procedures, and responsibilities, including those of the Data Intake Group. The working group's initial product, the June 2014 information governance policy, states that information to which access is restricted by law, including the Dodd-Frank restrictions, must be treated in accordance with such restrictions.[70] The policy also incorporates existing policies and lays out high-level principles, guidelines, and responsibilities for the intake, management (including storage, internal sharing and access, and use), disclosure, and disposition of information. However, the standards and written procedures to implement this policy are still under development, according to CFPB staff.

---

[70]This policy takes effect September 30, 2014.

Federal internal control standards and guidance discuss the importance of having written documentation and procedures for control activities.[71] CFPB staff said that in setting up the new agency, they emphasized adopting practices that help ensure that these issues were addressed but had not yet formally defined roles, responsibilities, and documentation requirements for the Data Intake Group in written procedures. Establishing such procedures for its data intake process will help CFPB ensure that staff consistently take appropriate steps when evaluating proposed data collections, including reviewing them to determine whether the Dodd-Frank restrictions apply.

CFPB Lacks Written Policies and Procedures for Anonymizing Data

In addition to Dodd-Frank restrictions that CFPB must follow, NIST guidance calls for agencies to minimize collection and use of personal information when possible. Although CFPB has taken steps to minimize use of information that directly identifies individuals in certain data collections, the agency has not developed standard policies and written procedures to document the practices it uses for anonymizing data, including clarifying how data sensitivity will be assessed and defining specific roles, responsibilities, and steps in accordance with NIST guidance and privacy controls. We found instances in which the agency failed to fully remove sensitive information in some of its data collections, as described below.

- **Data identifiability and sensitivity:** NIST recommends that agencies evaluate how easily data fields can be used to identify specific individuals, the sensitivity of individual data fields, and the sensitivity of groups of data fields.[72] Federal internal control standards also call for appropriate documentation of decisions and control activities.[73] According to CFPB staff, discussions among staff about removing sensitive data elements were informal and not documented. CFPB also has not specified in policy which data fields are considered sensitive or potentially identifying and should be removed or masked.

---

[71]GAO, *Standards for Internal Control in the Federal Government*, GAO/AIMD-00-21.3.1 (Washington, D.C.: November 1999) and *Internal Control Management and Evaluation Tool*, GAO-01-1008G (Washington, D.C.: August 2001).

[72]NIST SP 800-122.

[73]GAO/AIMD-00-21.3.1.

Our observation of files from two of the institutions providing deposit advance products data found that, although no individuals were directly identified in the files used for analysis, one file from one institution (with more than 1 million records) contained the nine-digit zip code for each record. According to CFPB staff, this information should not have been in that file. In the consumer credit data, CFPB procured the complete data package the credit reporting agency offered (a standard product), which included marketing data, without any personal identifiers. The marketing data contained demographic characteristics—including a religion variable that the credit reporting agency obtained or developed internally—on the sample of individuals whose credit record information CFPB obtained. When we observed an extract of the data with CFPB staff, we noted the existence of the religion variable. Not all CFPB staff realized the database contained that information. They said that CFPB considered this particular information sensitive and staff would remove it from their database. The Privacy Act generally prohibits federal agencies from maintaining records describing how any individual exercises rights guaranteed by the First Amendment.[74] However, as noted previously, to be a record under the Privacy Act, information about an individual must contain the person's name or other identifier, and the information CFPB acquired did not contain personal identifiers.

- **Minimization of personal information used in research:** NIST recommends that agencies (1) develop policies and procedures that minimize the use of personal information for research and other purposes and (2) implement controls to protect personal information used for research and other purposes.[75] However, CFPB staff said they have not developed written procedures for removing personal identifiers from supervisory data or implemented controls such as requiring reviews of anonymized files to ensure that all fields with information that directly identifies individuals had been removed.

CFPB staff said that they do not have written policies and procedures for anonymizing data—including documented assessments of the sensitivity of data elements and specific roles, responsibilities (including reviews), and steps—because they have made it clear to staff to maintain as little

---

[74]5 U.S.C. § 552a(e)(7).

[75]NIST SP 800-53, Revision 4.

personal information as possible and they expect staff to know which data elements are sensitive and should be removed. CFPB staff also said they had not performed formal assessments of the sensitivity of data elements because they have no plans to release such data publicly. However, some privacy experts have noted that re-identification of consumer financial data has become easier with the increase of online databases and the rise of "big data." For example, a recent report found that anonymization strategies used in the past may not be robust enough in light of current and emerging technology and techniques.[76] Some privacy experts have noted that only removing direct identifiers from a database generally does not sufficiently anonymize the data. However, two researchers noted that the risk of re-identifying data that have been properly anonymized likely is overstated because identifying large numbers of individuals in many anonymized data is difficult and takes specialized expertise.[77] Nevertheless, written policies and procedures for assessing the sensitivity of data fields and removing sensitive data fields would allow CFPB to comprehensively assess its data collections to help ensure they are sufficiently anonymized and contain no unnecessary sensitive information. In turn, such formal assessments would enhance CFPB's assurance that the privacy of the consumer financial data in its data collections has been adequately protected.

CFPB Lacks Written Procedures for Documenting Decisions for the Paperwork Reduction Act

CFPB has taken steps to comply with PRA requirements intended to minimize the burden of data collections and maximize the practical utility of the information collected. However, CFPB lacks written procedures for how its staff should document determinations of whether PRA applies to its data collections, including consultations with OMB. PRA generally requires federal agencies to seek and obtain OMB approval before undertaking an identical collection of information directed to 10 or more entities. OMB's PRA regulations also state that if a collection is addressed to all or a substantial majority of an industry, it is presumed to involve 10 or more entities and must follow PRA requirements.[78] For collections subject to PRA, agencies must seek comments from the public on the necessity of proposed collections, the accuracy of agencies'

---

[76]President's Council of Advisors on Science and Technology, *Report to the President: Big Data and Privacy: A Technological Perspective* (Washington, D.C.: May 2014).

[77]Ann Cavoukian and Daniel Castro, *Big Data and Innovation, Setting the Record Straight: De-identification Does Work* (Toronto, Ontario: June 16, 2014).

[78]5 C.F.R. § 1320.3(c)(4)(ii).

estimates of burden, ways to enhance the quality, utility, and clarity of the information collected, and ways to minimize the burden of the collection on respondents before submitting the proposal to OMB.

According to CFPB staff, at the time they began these various large-scale data collections, CFPB staff considered their contents and determined that, for two reasons, they did not need to seek formal OMB approval under PRA for these collections. First, CFPB procured much of the data from private companies that serve as information resellers. Such data are commercially available products and did not constitute information collections under PRA, according to CFPB staff. Second, when CFPB collected the information itself, staff said the agency did not ask exactly the same questions of more than nine financial institutions, which would have necessitated OMB approval.

But CFPB does not have written procedures for consistently and appropriately documenting PRA determinations (both internally and from OMB) for proposed collections. Instead, CFPB staff told us that initially colleagues with PRA expertise (PRA team) provided internal training on PRA, including the need to consult with the team and OMB staff about determinations. After the Data Intake Group was established in 2013, the PRA team began participating in the group's meetings to ensure discussions about PRA applicability and the need for OMB consultation took place. CFPB staff said that under current practice, staff from the PRA team who participate in the Data Intake Group complete a section of a worksheet to specify the number of respondents in the collection, the share of the market, whether OMB approval is required, and the status of OMB approval. E-mails that document the Data Intake Group decisions that we reviewed include information on whether the group determined that PRA applied, but do not specify whether OMB was consulted or the basis for determinations by the PRA team.

In the specific case of CFPB's credit card collection and its information-sharing agreement with OCC, CFPB did not have appropriate documentation of its consultations with OMB about PRA applicability. In 2012, CFPB sought to collect monthly account data from nine credit card issuers while also obtaining (through an information-sharing agreement) nearly identical data OCC had been collecting since 2009 from 9 different issuers. According to internal June 2012 e-mails that we reviewed, CFPB staff stated that by collecting information from 9 of more than 3,000 issuers, neither CFPB nor OCC were triggering PRA requirements under the "substantial majority of an industry" standard in OMB regulations. These e-mails also indicated that CFPB staff had discussed with OCC whether PRA approval from OMB was needed and learned that OCC had not sought OMB approval for its ongoing collection.

In the same e-mails from June 2012, the CFPB PRA team reported that OMB had said (1) CFPB could collect information from nine banks, (2) OCC could continue to collect information from another nine banks, and (3) OCC could share its data with CFPB without going through the PRA process. CFPB staff told us that they did not obtain documentation from OMB staff because the advice had been received by telephone. However, OMB staff with whom we spoke said that they were not aware of either CFPB's or OCC's credit card collections and did not recall a discussion with CFPB about its collection. OMB staff also could not find documentation of such a discussion, although they acknowledged that informal telephone consultations generally are not documented. Furthermore, OMB staff told us that an information-sharing agreement that could result in agencies bypassing the requirements of PRA—in particular, the public notice and comment provisions—by collecting data from more than nine entities would warrant closer examination to ensure PRA compliance. They added that OMB would want to assess whether these collections met the "substantial majority of an industry" standard, which also would necessitate the need for a formal PRA review.

Federal internal control standards call for appropriate documentation of decisions and control activities.[79] In the initial period of agency operations, CFPB staff said they emphasized complying with the requirements over documenting decisions and establishing written procedures. However, without written procedures for consistently and appropriately documenting PRA-related decisions and discussions with OMB, including about the credit card collection and information-sharing agreement, CFPB lacks reasonable assurance that its collections are conducted in compliance with requirements intended to help avoid inefficiencies and minimize burden.

In our review of OCC's collections of credit card and mortgage data, we found information indicating that OCC was now obtaining data from more than nine entities in these collections, which would require OMB approval. OCC began collecting credit card data from nine institutions in 2009, and OCC staff told us that they had determined that they did not need an

---

[79]GAO/AIMD-00-21.3.1.

OMB PRA review because they were obtaining data from fewer than 10 institutions. In addition, OCC reported that the nine institutions represented less than 1 percent of all national banks and federal savings associations, which therefore did not meet the "majority of the industry" provision in OMB's regulations. However, in the information-sharing agreement with CFPB, OCC listed nine entities as "reporters" (reporting institution) for the credit card collection, but also indicated several instances in which two or more national banks that were part of the same holding company were combined into a single "reporter." After our analysis showed that OCC had data from more than nine entities, OCC staff told us they reviewed the information requests they had sent to financial institutions and confirmed the requests were sent to institutions beyond the original nine. They said that as of July 2014, 16 entities were providing credit card data to OCC. As a result, they planned to submit the collection to OMB for approval under PRA. In addition, after reviewing OCC's information-sharing agreement with the Federal Reserve for its first-lien mortgage and home equity data collections, we found that OCC was collecting data from 61 entities for first-lien mortgage data, and 64 entities for home equity data. On September 5, 2014, OCC published notices in the *Federal Register* describing these collections in advance of submitting them to OMB for approval.[80] Until completing steps to obtain OMB's approval for each of these three data collections, OCC will lack reasonable assurance that the collections are in compliance with statutory requirements intended to minimize burden on the financial institutions and maximize the practical utility of the information collected.

CFPB Generally Met Statutory Privacy Requirements, but Lacked Elements of Certain Recommended Privacy Controls

CFPB has taken steps to comply with other requirements and recommended controls aimed at protecting the privacy of personal information that include publishing notices about information collections and adopting policies. Beyond the specific Dodd-Frank requirements and general PRA requirements, CFPB also is subject to the Privacy Act and the privacy provisions of the E-Government Act, which require all federal agencies to conduct certain steps when collecting data that includes personal or direct identifiers of individuals.[81] CFPB follows NIST guidance

---

[80]79 Fed. Reg. 53,101 (Sept. 5, 2014) (credit card data); 79 Fed. Reg. 53,102 (Sept. 5, 2014) (home equity lending data); 79 Fed. Reg. 53,103 (Sept. 5, 2014) (first-lien residential mortgage data).

[81]As mentioned earlier, the Dodd-Frank Act also requires that CFPB take steps to ensure that certain information, including personal information, is not disclosed to the public when such information is protected by law. 12 U.S.C. § 5512(c)(8).

in implementing privacy controls, which are designed to facilitate compliance with these statutes.[82]

Privacy Act Requirements

CFPB has published notices as required under the Privacy Act, which is intended to regulate agencies' collection, maintenance, use, and dissemination of information about individuals. Under the Privacy Act, federal agencies must publish system of records notices (SORN) in the *Federal Register* if they plan to maintain, collect, use, or disseminate records about individuals that are retrieved from a system of records by the name of an individual or other personal identifier.[83] Such notices also are required for systems of records operated by contractors on behalf of an agency.

According to CFPB staff, most of CFPB's consumer financial data collections are not a system of records and do not require the issuance of a SORN because the data are not typically retrieved by personal identifiers, which is necessary for the information to be covered by the Privacy Act.[84] However, CFPB issued three SORNs relevant to our review that provide public notice covering other information the agency obtains during the course of its operations and which its staff may at times retrieve using personal identifiers.[85] Two of the SORNs (both published in August 2011) are for its supervision databases, which cover data collected from and about the depository and nondepository institutions CFPB supervises.[86] The third SORN (published in November 2012)

---

[82]NIST SP 800-53, Revision 4.

[83]SORNs must identify the type of data collected, the types of individuals about whom information is collected, and procedures that individuals can use to review and correct personal information.

[84]Two supervisory collections—for deposit advance products and storefront payday loans—included personal identifiers when CFPB obtained them from financial institutions. CFPB officials stated that the records are not retrieved by identifiers and therefore do not meet the Privacy Act definition of a system of records. However, if CFPB's use of this information changed so that records were retrieved by personal identifiers, officials said the deposit advance products dataset would be covered by the SORN for the depository institution supervision database, and the payday loans dataset would be covered by the SORN for the nondepository supervision database.

[85]A list of all CFPB's SORNs is available on CFPB's website, accessed on July 25, 2014 at http://www.consumerfinance.gov/privacy/.

[86]76 Fed. Reg. 45,761 (Aug. 1, 2011) (nondepository supervision); 76 Fed. Reg. 45,765 (Aug. 1, 2011) (depository institution supervision).

covers market and consumer research records.[87] Consistent with the Privacy Act, the SORNs included a general description of CFPB's authority and purpose for collecting and using personal information and how individuals could access and correct information maintained about them. The inclusion of these elements is also consistent with NIST privacy controls.[88] CFPB staff told us that the SORNs were published before CFPB collected information maintained in these systems.

While most CFPB data collections likely do not constitute systems of records, agency staff said other activities involving personal information, such as matching across databases, also were covered by the SORNs they had issued. For example, CFPB staff said that a matching process conducted by a third party on behalf of CFPB on the credit card data uses personal identifiers obtained from supervised depository institutions to retrieve records in the third party's system. To the extent this matching process creates a temporary system of records by virtue of retrieving the records by personal identifiers, CFPB staff told us the need for public notice is met by the SORN issued for the depository institution supervision database. According to CFPB staff, the third party immediately removes all identifiers once the records have been matched and then transmits the resulting database to CFPB's contractor, which transmits the data to CFPB. Staff said that neither CFPB nor its contractor retrieves records in the database by personal identifier and therefore the database CFPB maintains does not constitute a system of records under the Privacy Act.

E-Government Act Requirements

The E-Government Act has provisions that require federal agencies to review data to help ensure sufficient protections for the privacy of personal information held electronically. Federal agencies subject to this

---

[87]77 Fed. Reg. 67,802 (Nov. 14, 2012). According to the SORN, these records include information collected from consumers as well as from providers of consumer financial products and services, consumer reporting agencies, government entities, and commercial and nonprofit entities that compile datasets from one or more of these sources.

[88]NIST SP 800-53, Revision 4. The NIST privacy control for "authority to collect" calls for an organization to determine and document the legal authority that permits the collection, use, and maintenance of personal information. The "purpose specification" control calls for an organization to describe the purposes for which personal information is collected, used, maintained, and shared. The "individual access" control calls for an organization to publish access procedures in SORNs. The "system of records notices and Privacy Act statements" control calls for an organization to publish SORNs in the *Federal Register*.

act must conduct privacy impact assessments (PIA) that analyze how personal information is collected, stored, shared, and managed in their information systems. Agencies must make PIAs public to the extent practicable, although this requirement can be modified or waived for security reasons or to protect sensitive or private information.[89] To comply with these requirements, in June 2013 CFPB prepared a PIA for its "Cloud 1" general support system (GSS), the information system in which it maintains its consumer financial data collections.[90] The agency completed the PIA (which has not been made public) as part of the security assessment and authorization process for the GSS. However, we found that the PIA discussed consumer financial data very generally and contained few details about the privacy risks raised by collections of consumer financial data.

After completing the GSS PIA, CFPB staff said that they subsequently changed the focus of PIAs from assessments of information systems to assessments of categories of data collections. They said this change would provide clearer information to the public about privacy risks for specific data collections. As part of this new privacy analysis, they published a PIA for market analysis of administrative data under research authorities in December 2013 and another PIA covering the use of supervisory data for market research in July 2014.[91] Both PIAs note that re-identification of individuals is a risk posed by the data collections. However, in both PIAs CFPB states that its staff will not attempt to re-identify individuals in databases that are anonymized. In addition, CFPB is contractually prohibited from attempting to re-identify individuals in at

---

[89]CFPB adopted a formal PIA policy in June 2014 (effective December 2014) that defines roles and responsibilities for conducting PIAs and helps to ensure compliance with the requirements of the E-Government Act and OMB guidance.

[90]CFPB also published system-level PIAs for the Scheduling and Examination System (also referred to as the Supervision and Examination System) in May 2012 and the Compliance Analysis Toolkit (supervisory tool) in October 2012. These systems may contain datasets provided by financial institutions to CFPB during the course of supervisory examination activities, but according to CFPB staff, staff who work on large-scale data collections cannot access these datasets in these systems.

[91]Consumer Financial Protection Bureau, *Privacy Impact Assessment: Market Analysis of Administrative Data Under Research Authorities* (Washington, D.C.: Dec. 20, 2013) and Consumer Financial Protection Bureau, *Privacy Impact Assessment: Certain Supervision, Enforcement, and Fair Lending (SEFL) Data Used for Market Research* (Washington, D.C.: July 14, 2014).

least one data collection procured from a contractor. Table 4 summarizes which of CFPB's data collections are covered by PIAs.

Table 4: CFPB Data Collections and Associated Privacy Impact Assessments (PIA), as of July 2014

Data collection	Directly identifies individuals?	PIA conducted?	Name of PIA that currently applies[a]
Arbitration case records	✓	✓	*Market Analysis of Administrative Data Under Research Authorities*, December 2013
Automobile sales	NA	NA	NA[b]
Consumer credit report information		✓	*Market Analysis of Administrative Data Under Research Authorities*, December 2013
Credit cards		✓	*Certain Supervision, Enforcement, and Fair Lending (SEFL) Data Used for Market Research*, July 2014
Credit scores		✓	*Market Analysis of Administrative Data Under Research Authorities*, December 2013
Deposit advance products	✓[c]	✓	*Certain Supervision, Enforcement, and Fair Lending (SEFL) Data Used for Market Research*, July 2014
Mortgages		✓	*Market Analysis of Administrative Data Under Research Authorities*, December 2013
Private-label mortgages		✓	*Market Analysis of Administrative Data Under Research Authorities*, December 2013
Online payday loans		✓	*Market Analysis of Administrative Data Under Research Authorities*, December 2013
Overdraft fees		✓	*Certain Supervision, Enforcement, and Fair Lending (SEFL) Data Used for Market Research*, July 2014
Private student loans		✓	*Market Analysis of Administrative Data Under Research Authorities*, December 2013
Storefront payday loans	✓[c]	✓	*Certain Supervision, Enforcement, and Fair Lending (SEFL) Data Used for Market Research*, July 2014

Sources: GAO analysis of CFPB information. | GAO-14-758

[a]According to CFPB officials, CFPB initially complied with requirements to issue PIAs through system-level PIAs (such as a PIA for its general support system) that covered data collections stored in those systems. However, not all the system-level PIAs were made public.

[b]According to CFPB staff, no PIA was required for this collection.

[c]As discussed previously, CFPB removed information that directly identifies individuals from the files staff use to analyze these data.

NIST Privacy Controls

CFPB has implemented certain controls intended to ensure the proper treatment of consumer financial data obtained, but CFPB has not yet developed documentation or implemented plans, procedures, programs, and training as specified in several controls. NIST's guidance includes controls for protecting privacy and ensuring the proper handling of personal information.[92] CFPB has taken actions to address many of the NIST-recommended controls, including the following:

- **Data quality and integrity:** CFPB included data quality provisions in its contract with the aggregator for the credit card data collection. These provisions outlined quality assurance steps for the aggregator to take to help ensure the accuracy and completeness of the information the credit card issuers provided. In addition, CFPB has issued information quality guidelines for information it publishes. These steps are consistent with control steps calling for an organization to check for (and correct as necessary) inaccurate information and issue guidelines maximizing the quality, utility, objectivity, and integrity of disseminated information.

- **Security:** CFPB has adopted a privacy incident response plan and standard operating procedures for such incidents. The privacy incident response plan included most of the components recommended by NIST: the establishment of a privacy incident response team; a process to determine whether notice to oversight organizations or affected individuals is appropriate; a process to assess the privacy risk posed by the incident; and internal procedures to ensure prompt reporting by employees and contractors of any privacy incident to appropriate officials.[93] The CFPB privacy team has created a log for privacy incidents and completed after-action reports that detail what was reported, what the investigation found, and what steps were taken. These steps are consistent with the control for an organization to develop and implement a privacy incident response plan and provide an organized and effective response to privacy incidents in accordance with the plan.

- **Use limitation:** CFPB has entered into MOUs with federal and state agencies, which describe the purposes for which personal information (and other nonpublic information) may be used by receiving parties.

---

[92]NIST SP 800-53, Revision 4.

[93]NIST guidance includes one additional step that CFPB's privacy incident response plan does not include: internal procedures for reporting noncompliance with organizational privacy policy by employees or contractors to appropriate management or oversight officials. CFPB staff said they are told in privacy training to report noncompliance with CFPB's privacy policy and that the process is the same as for reporting privacy incidents.

CFPB also developed a policy for staff that governs when confidential information may be shared with external parties. These steps are consistent with control steps for information sharing with third parties, which call for an organization to enter into MOUs that specify the personal information covered and enumerate the purposes for which it may be used.

- **Accountability, audit, and risk management:** CFPB has outlined privacy roles, responsibilities (which include safeguarding nonpublic, business-sensitive, confidential, or personal information or data), and access requirements for all CFPB contractors and service providers in various policy documents. General privacy and confidentiality clauses were included in several contracts we reviewed. CFPB subsequently prepared guidance for its staff on privacy-specific clauses to be included in data collection and analysis contracts. In addition, members of the Data Intake Group review contracts to help ensure that contracts for collections that include personal information are flagged to include appropriate privacy clauses. These steps are consistent with the control for an organization to establish privacy roles, responsibilities, and access requirements for contractors and service providers, and to include privacy requirements in contracts and other acquisition-related documents.

However, CFPB does not yet have (1) a comprehensive privacy plan incorporating its various privacy policies and guidance; (2) a documented privacy risk management process; (3) a comprehensive, documented program for monitoring and auditing privacy controls or a regularly scheduled independent review of its program; and (4) role-based privacy training, as specified in other controls relating to accountability, audit, and risk management.

- **Comprehensive privacy plan:** NIST's "governance and privacy program" control calls for agencies to develop a strategic organizational plan for implementing applicable privacy controls, policies, and procedures. CFPB has developed a number of privacy policies and guidance documents, including a high-level privacy policy, a handbook for sensitive information, a PIA policy (which takes effect in December 2014), a PIA template, and guidance for preparing SORNs. However, CFPB privacy staff stated that they had not yet brought them together to develop a comprehensive plan that covers all of CFPB's privacy operations.

- **Documented privacy risk-management process:** NIST's "privacy impact and risk assessment" control calls for agencies to document and implement a process for privacy risk management that assesses risks to individuals resulting from collecting, sharing, storing, transmitting, using, and disposing of personal information. Agencies also should conduct PIAs for information systems, programs, or other activities that pose a privacy risk in accordance with applicable law, OMB policy, or organizational policies or procedures. Supplemental guidance for this control states that tools and processes for managing risk "include, but are not limited to, the conduct of PIAs." We reported on the importance of assessing privacy risks to help program managers and system owners determine appropriate policies and techniques to implement the policies.[94] Currently, CFPB follows an informal process for managing privacy risks that does not fully document risks involved with data collections or the methods CFPB plans to use to address the risks. CFPB staff stated that the agency has centralized all privacy activities with the Chief Privacy Officer and a team of CFPB staff (privacy team), who perform all assessments of privacy risks, primarily through the PIA process. In June 2014, CFPB adopted a formal PIA policy that will take effect in December 2014 and that places responsibility with the Chief Privacy Officer for determining whether PIAs are required. But the policy does not specify the procedures to be used and documentation required for making such determinations. CFPB staff said that privacy team representatives to the Data Intake Group currently use a worksheet to assess and document whether proposed collections require a PIA and whether an existing PIA would cover the collections. The privacy team follows CFPB's PIA template to create new PIAs. However, CFPB staff said there are no written procedures they follow to guide their assessments, although such procedures are being developed. CFPB staff were not always able to clearly identify whether a specific data collection required a PIA and if so, which one, because these prior determinations had not been documented. Furthermore, staff said they do not document discussions or analyses that lead to the conclusions published in their PIAs.

- **Comprehensive, documented program for monitoring and auditing privacy controls:** According to NIST's "privacy monitoring and auditing" control, agencies are to monitor and audit privacy controls and internal privacy policy to ensure effective implementation.

---

[94]GAO, *Privacy: OPM Should Better Monitor Implementation of Privacy-Related Policies and Procedures for Background Investigations*, GAO-10-849 (Washington, D.C.: Sept. 7, 2010).

NIST guidance calls for regular assessments and mentions external audits as means to obtain these assessments. CFPB is required to have an annual independent audit of its operations and budget.[95] CFPB identified the areas that the auditor reviewed and selected its privacy programs, policies, and processes as one of the areas for review in 2012. In its 2012 report, CFPB's independent auditor identified the lack of a formal privacy compliance program as an opportunity to improve performance.[96] CFPB staff said they had addressed this finding, noting their policy for annually reviewing SORNs and PIAs and a worksheet CFPB prepared for an information technology application that lists the NIST privacy controls and the steps CFPB had taken to implement them. CFPB staff said they planned to complete similar worksheets for each new application and system. However, staff do not plan to prepare such worksheets for applications and systems already in place, and have not established procedures for reviewing and updating the worksheets. Although CFPB has adopted a checklist for reviewing SORNs, staff said they do not have a similar checklist or documentation requirements for reviewing PIAs. In addition, CFPB staff said they had not had an external audit of their privacy practices other than the 2012 audit.

- **Role-based privacy training:** NIST's "privacy awareness and training" control calls for agencies to administer targeted, role-based privacy training (in addition to basic privacy training that all staff receive) for personnel having responsibility for personal information or for activities that involve personal information. CFPB has developed a training process for privacy awareness, and CFPB employees and contractors receive privacy training as part of annual security awareness training. CFPB also trains staff on the treatment of confidential supervisory information, which may contain consumers' personal information. CFPB staff said they adopted organization-wide privacy awareness training from the Department of the Treasury, but were still developing role-based privacy training and did not yet have an estimated date for completion.

---

[95]ASR Analytics performed the independent audits for 2011 and 2012. KPMG performed the independent audit for 2013. In addition to the independent audits of CFPB's operations and budget, we are required to audit CFPB's financial statements each year.

[96]ASR Analytics, *Independent Performance Audit of CFPB Operations and Budget* (Potomac, Md.: Nov. 13, 2012).

CFPB staff said that, in setting up the new agency, they had adopted policies and practices that would address privacy issues. However, the agency has not yet comprehensively documented its policies and procedures or completed development of its role-based privacy training. By not fully implementing controls to include written procedures, comprehensive documentation, a regular review of its privacy practices, and targeted training, CFPB is hampered in its ability to identify and monitor privacy risks and ensure the proper handling of personal information.

CFPB Has Implemented Information Security Measures to Protect Consumer Financial Data, but Weaknesses Exist

CFPB has taken actions to protect the consumer financial data it has collected from unauthorized disclosure, but some documentation lacked key information and its evaluation of how a service provider protects data was not comprehensive. CFPB has established an information security program, implemented controls to protect access to sensitive data, and assessed the risks of its consumer financial data collections using a risk-management framework that adhered to federal information security guidance. However, CFPB's documentation of its risk assessments and remedial action plans to correct identified weaknesses for the information system and related components that maintain and process consumer financial data lacked key elements. Further, the initial evaluation CFPB had completed of its service provider was not sufficiently comprehensive.

CFPB Established an Information Security Program

In a 2013 audit of the CFPB's information security program, the Office of Inspector General (OIG) for the Federal Reserve and CFPB determined that CFPB had taken multiple steps, consistent with FISMA requirements, to develop, document, and implement an information security program.[97] FISMA requires agencies to develop, document, and implement an information security program. OMB and the Department of Homeland Security (DHS) have instructed agencies to report annually on a variety of metrics, which are used to gauge implementation of information security

---

[97] Board of Governors of the Federal Reserve System, Consumer Financial Protection Bureau, Office of Inspector General, *2013 Audit of the CFPB's Information Security Program*, 2013-IT-C-020 (Washington, D.C.: Dec. 2, 2013).

programs.[98] The OIG reported that CFPB's overall information security program in 2013 was generally consistent with requirements in 6 of 11 information security areas outlined in DHS reporting instructions: (1) identity and access management; (2) incident response and reporting; (3) risk management; (4) plan of action and milestones; (5) remote access management; and (6) contractor systems. For a seventh area—security capital planning—the OIG noted that CFPB has been taking sufficient actions to establish a security capital planning program in accordance with DHS requirements.

The OIG identified several opportunities to improve CFPB's information security program through automation, centralization, and other enhancements. Specifically, the agency had not defined metrics to facilitate decision-making and improve performance of its information security continuous monitoring program; implemented tools to more comprehensively assess security controls and system configurations; developed and implemented an organization-wide configuration management plan and consistent process for patch management; designed, developed, and implemented a role-based training program for individuals with significant security responsibilities; or fully implemented a capability to centrally track, analyze, and correlate audit log and incident information. In addition, CFPB's contingency planning for a selected system needed improvement. The OIG made four recommendations to address these issues, with which CFPB concurred. The OIG noted that CFPB's planned actions were responsive to the recommendations, but as of July 2014, the recommendations remained open pending the OIG's review during the 2014 FISMA audit.

CFPB Established Access Controls for Protecting Consumer Financial Data

CFPB had implemented several logical access controls for the component of the information system that maintains the consumer financial data collections we reviewed and was scanning for problems or vulnerabilities. Agencies can protect the resources that support their critical operations from unauthorized access by designing and implementing controls intended to prevent, limit, and detect unauthorized

---

[98]In 2010, an OMB memorandum assigned DHS primary responsibility for the operational aspects of cybersecurity, subject to OMB oversight. DHS has been responsible for assisting OMB in overseeing executive branch agencies' compliance with FISMA, overseeing cybersecurity operations, and providing related assistance. See OMB, *Clarifying Cybersecurity Responsibilities and Activities of the Executive Office of the President and the Department of Homeland Security (DHS)*, OMB Memorandum M-10-28 (Washington, D.C.: July 6, 2010).

access to computing resources, programs, information, and facilities. Inadequate access controls diminish the reliability of computerized information and increase the risk of unauthorized disclosure, modification, and destruction of sensitive information and disruption of service. As part of assessing the controls that CFPB uses to protect consumer financial data it collects, we reviewed the logical access controls the agency implemented on the primary servers that staff use to process and store these data. As one of the ways CFPB seeks to mitigate the risk of unauthorized re-identification of individuals, the agency has controlled which staff have access to data collections that directly identify individuals.

Based on interviews with CFPB staff who manage these servers and observations and reviews of information technology security controls and settings we determined that CFPB had installed and configured automated tools to perform regular configuration management and periodic security scans of the servers supporting the component. CFPB also leveraged its existing centralized account management system to manage who had access to these servers. The agency also had implemented controls intended to prevent staff members who are not on the approved list from accessing consumer financial data. According to CFPB, there have been no security incidents resulting in unauthorized disclosures of information in the information system component that maintains consumer financial data.

In July 2014, the Federal Reserve and CFPB OIG issued a report on a review of the cloud-based system in which CFPB maintains its consumer financial data collections.[99] The OIG made recommendations to address weaknesses they identified in work conducted in fall 2013, including recommending improvements to CFPB's procedures for system and information integrity and configuration management. OIG staff told us that CFPB has implemented corrections in these areas. The OIG report also recommended that CFPB take actions related to contingency planning and incident response; CFPB actions to address these were still underway.

---

[99]Board of Governors of the Federal Reserve System, Consumer Financial Protection Bureau, Office of Inspector General, *Security Control Review of the CFPB's Cloud Computing–Based General Support System,* 2014-IT-C-010 (Washington, D.C.: July 17, 2014).

CFPB Generally Followed Steps of the NIST Risk Management Framework for the System That Maintains Consumer Financial Data

Although the collection of consumer financial data can create concerns over improper use or unauthorized disclosure, CFPB has taken steps to assess the risks posed by these data and implemented controls or taken other actions to address the risks. NIST has published a risk-management framework, which recommends that agencies follow a six-step process involving (1) security categorization; (2) security control selection; (3) security control implementation; (4) security control assessment; (5) information system authorization; and (6) security control monitoring.[100] The framework integrates information security and risk-management activities into the system development life-cycle.

CFPB has adopted this framework as the basis for the process it uses to assess the risks of the consumer financial data and other data it collects and generally applied the framework to the information system and related components that maintain, process, and store the consumer financial data collections we reviewed. To address the steps of the risk-management framework, CFPB generally completed information security documentation required by FISMA (such as risk assessments, system security plans, and remedial action plans) or outlined in NIST guidance (including security assessment plans and reports) to address the steps of the risk management framework. Table 5 provides additional information on CFPB's actions to implement the framework for the information system and its components.

Table 5: CFPB's Implementation of the NIST Risk Management Framework for the System and Related Components That Maintain Consumer Financial Data, as of July 1, 2014

NIST risk management framework steps	CFPB actions
Step 1: Security categorization	• Categorized its information system and related component, which maintains and processes consumer financial data, in accordance with the Federal Information Processing Standards, and documented the security categorization in the system security plan[a] Specifically, the categorization decision for the system was reviewed and approved in July 2013. • Documented the information system description (including the system boundary) and the system categorization decision in the system security plan.

---

[100]NIST SP 800-37, Revision 1.

NIST risk management framework steps	CFPB actions
Step 2: Security control selection	• Selected security controls for its system that maintains and processes consumer financial data, and documented them in the system security plan. Security control selections were consistent with NIST guidance for the system categorization and documented in the system security plan.
	• Developed and documented a continuous monitoring program, which includes a strategy that describes the specific controls to be tested, the frequency of monitoring each control, and a method for reporting the results.
Step 3: Security control implementation	• Documented the implementation status of selected security controls, including steps to implement each control, in the system security plan. CFPB's system security plan for the system that maintains and processes consumer financial data included 15 of the 17 applicable elements suggested by NIST guidance.
• Step 4: Security control assessment	• Developed a security assessment plan for its system that maintains and processes consumer financial data, and recorded the testing that was done in accordance with the plan.
	• Documented the results of its security assessment in a security assessment report dated July 2013. The security assessment report included 9 of 11 applicable elements suggested in NIST guidance.
• Step 5: Information system authorization	• Developed remedial action plans for its system and related components that maintain and process consumer financial data.
	• Conducted risk assessments on its system and related components that maintain and process consumer financial data.
	• Assigned an authorizing official for its system and related components that maintain and process consumer financial data, who granted the system an authority to operate in July 2013.
• Step 6: Security control monitoring	• Conducted security control monitoring of its system and related components that maintain and process consumer financial data. Specifically, CFPB tested selected security controls specified in its continuous monitoring strategy and documented the results in a continuous monitoring report.

Source: GAO analysis of CFPB documentation. | GAO-14-758

[a]NIST's Standards for Security Categorization of Federal Information and Information Systems (Federal Information Processing Standards Publication 199) defines three levels of impacts on organizational operations and assets or individuals resulting from the loss of confidentiality, integrity, or availability: low, at which such losses could be expected to have a limited adverse effect; moderate, at which such losses could be expected to have a serious adverse effect; and high, at which such losses could be expected to have a severe or catastrophic adverse effect.

CFPB's Information Security Documentation Lacked Key Elements

Although CFPB generally completed the information security documentation required by FISMA or outlined in NIST guidance for implementing the risk management framework, several key elements were missing from various documents. NIST has issued guidance for conducting risk assessments that outline elements that should be included in documentation of risk assessment results. In addition, CFPB adopted a risk management process and guidance for preparing remedial action plans that outline its internal documentation requirements.

| Risk Assessments | Conducting and documenting risk assessments help ensure agencies fully assess the risks of data they maintain and apply appropriate protections, but CFPB's risk assessment documentation did not include all the elements NIST guidance recommends for communicating results of risk assessments. Specifically, the three risk assessment and recommendation forms we reviewed did not include the following essential elements identified by NIST: (1) the assumptions and constraints under which the risk assessment was conducted; (2) information sources to be used in the assessment; (3) the risk model and analytical approach used in the risk assessment; (4) threat sources; (5) potential threat events; (6) vulnerabilities and predisposing conditions that affect the likelihood that potential threat events will result in adverse impacts; (7) the likelihood that potential threat events will result in adverse impacts; (8) the adverse impacts from potential threat events; and (9) the risk to the organization from threat events.[101] The results of a fourth risk assessment were documented in a security assessment report. Although the security assessment report identified the assumptions and constraints under which the risk assessment was conducted and the risk model that was used (elements 1 and part of 3 above), it did not include the other elements listed above.

Enhancing its documentation of risk assessment results to be more comprehensive and consistent would help CFPB demonstrate that it has effectively assessed risk and identified and considered all threats and vulnerabilities to its operations. |
| Remedial Action Plans | Remedial action plans can assist agencies in tracking and ensuring that information security weaknesses are addressed in a timely way. However, CFPB's remedial action plans did not always include all the weaknesses identified. CFPB policy states that weaknesses identified during internal and external system reviews should be included in remedial action plans. We compared the CFPB system documentation and testing results with the remedial action plans for the information system and related components that maintain consumer financial data and found instances in which not all security weaknesses identified were included in the plans. For example, the system documentation for its information system identified 20 controls we reviewed that were not fully |

---

[101]NIST, *Guide for Conducting Risk Assessments*, Special Publication (SP) 800-30 (Gaithersburg, Md.: September 2012).

implemented—16 were listed as partially implemented, 3 were listed as planned for implementation, and 1 was listed as a new control. However, the 3 planned controls and 1 new control were not recorded in the system's remedial action plan.

In addition, CFPB had not remediated all weaknesses in its remedial action plans by their scheduled completion date in accordance with CFPB guidance. CFPB guidance included required completion dates for remediating all high-risk weaknesses (within 30 days), all medium-risk weaknesses (within 90 days), and all low-risk weaknesses (by the scheduled completion date documented in the remedial action plan). In addition, CFPB guidance states that staff should assign scheduled completion dates, which may extend beyond the required completion dates, based on realistic timelines given agency priorities and available resources. Of the 16 partially implemented controls we reviewed that were recorded as weaknesses in the remedial action plan, CFPB had not completed remedial steps for 9 weaknesses by the scheduled completion date of September 2013. Further, the scheduled completion dates had not been updated to reflect current plans for remediation. CFPB's testing of one of the system components that maintains and processes consumer financial data identified three high-risk weaknesses that were scheduled to be remediated by October 2013. One weakness was the aggregate risk posed by numerous medium- and low-risk findings identified during testing and automated scans. The remedial action plan required CFPB to analyze each finding to determine its risk impact and prioritize them for remediation or mitigation. According to the Chief Information Security Officer, CFPB has been making steady progress towards remediating the findings that make up this high-risk weakness; however, as of June 2014, CFPB had not addressed all these findings or updated the scheduled completion date in the remedial action plan to reflect the current timeline for completing these actions.

Ensuring that its remedial action plans are comprehensive and updated to reflect current timeframes for remediating weaknesses would enhance CFPB's ability to identify, assess, prioritize, and monitor the progress of corrective efforts for security weaknesses.

CFPB Developed a Process for Evaluating Service Providers but Initial Assessments Were Not Comprehensive

Under the FISMA information security program, agencies are required to develop a risk-management process that helps ensure that information and information systems provided or managed by another agency, contractor, or other source are protected with appropriate information security controls. CFPB has developed a risk management process that covers all agreements and contracts between CFPB and service providers that process information on its behalf. One step in the process is conducting assessments of these service providers based on the types of applications, tools, or services provided. Once the appropriate assessment is conducted, CFPB generates a risk assessment and recommendation form, including appropriate risk mitigation activities. The form is then submitted to the appropriate approval authorities. CFPB also tracks the implementation of its recommendations by creating risk mitigation items and activities that will be tracked through CFPB's remedial action plans.

Some actions have been taken to assess whether the service provider that processes consumer financial data on CFPB's behalf was implementing adequate protections. We reviewed a 2012 report by the service provider's independent auditor about certain controls the provider had in place. The independent auditor found the controls were suitably designed to provide reasonable assurance that control objectives would be achieved and that the tested controls were operating effectively throughout the review period. Officials from the provider told us that other federal agencies for which they process data also have reviewed their information security program. In addition, they said they had never had a breach of the environment in which they process and maintain CFPB's data. CFPB also conducted an initial review of this service provider to assess the risks associated with utilizing the providers' systems and services, and documented the findings and recommendations, which were reviewed and approved in March 2014. CFPB's contract with the service provider includes specific information security requirements and states that CFPB shall conduct annual reviews to help ensure security requirements in the contract are implemented, enforced, effective, and operating as intended. However, CFPB did not examine how the provider had implemented these requirements as part of its initial review of this provider.

Without effectively reviewing its service provider and following its own process of tracking risk mitigation items and activities, CFPB lacks assurance that it is fully safeguarding its information resources and making fully informed decisions related to managing risk and implementing risk mitigation controls.

Conclusions

To better detect risks in consumer financial markets and improve federal oversight of consumer financial protection laws, CFPB has collected consumer financial data on products ranging from credit card accounts to payday loans. CFPB has used the consumer financial data it collects to inform required rulemakings, develop examination strategies, and issue congressionally mandated reports. Recognizing the sensitivity of some of the consumer financial data it has collected, CFPB has taken steps to protect and secure these data collections, including adopting high-level privacy and security policies and processes. For example, the agency created a data intake process that brings together staff with relevant expertise to consider the statutory, privacy, and information security implications of proposals to collect consumer financial data. Staff also described a process for anonymizing large-scale data collections that directly identify individuals. In addition, CFPB recently developed overarching policies on information governance and privacy impact assessments.

However, CFPB staff said they were primarily focused on taking necessary actions to effectively carry out their mission during these early years of agency operations and as a result, a number of policies and processes were not fully documented or implemented, as required by federal internal control guidelines or outlined in NIST guidance. In particular:

- **Lack of written procedures:** CFPB lacks written procedures for its data intake process, including for evaluating whether statutory restrictions related to collecting personally identifiable financial information apply to large-scale data collections, documenting determinations of whether these collections are subject to PRA, and assessing and managing privacy risks of these collections. CFPB has not established written procedures for anonymizing data collections to help ensure staff take the appropriate steps each time or for monitoring and auditing privacy controls. In addition, CFPB did not consistently or comprehensively document its information security risk-assessment results. Developing written procedures with consistent, comprehensive documentation requirements would help provide CFPB with reasonable assurance that its collections comply with statutory requirements and that it will not place consumers' privacy at risk.

- **Incomplete implementation of privacy and security steps:** CFPB has not yet developed a comprehensive privacy plan that brings together existing policies and guidance. It has not established a regular schedule of periodic reviews of its privacy program, or completed development of a role-based privacy training program. CFPB also did not capture all information security weaknesses identified in its remedial action plans or update the plans to include current planned dates for remediation based on priorities and available resources. In addition, CFPB did not comprehensively evaluate the service provider that processes consumer financial data on its behalf for compliance with contract provisions. Taking these actions will help strengthen CFPB's privacy program and enhance its ability to identify, track, and mitigate security risks to consumer financial data stored on its systems.

- **Insufficient efforts on PRA compliance:** CFPB did not sufficiently document its consultation with OMB about the information-sharing agreement with OCC relating to the agencies' separate credit card collections and the implications under PRA, and OMB staff told us it warranted further review. OCC also had not sought OMB approval for its credit card and mortgage data collections even though it now obtains data from more than nine entities for each of these collections. Obtaining further guidance from OMB on whether the information-sharing agreement requires CFPB and OCC to follow procedures outlined in PRA and getting OMB approval for OCC's credit card and mortgage data collections would help both agencies ensure they fully comply with the law, do not unduly burden financial institutions, and maximize the practical utility of the information collected.

Recommendations for Executive Action

To help improve CFPB's efforts to protect and secure collected consumer financial data, we are making the following 11 recommendations to the Director of CFPB.

- To help ensure consistent implementation of its current processes and practices, the Director of CFPB should establish or enhance written procedures for:

  1. the data intake process, including reviews of proposed data collections for compliance applicable legal requirements and restrictions and documentation requirements for consultations with OMB about PRA applicability;

  2. anonymizing data, including how staff should assess data sensitivity, which steps to take to anonymize data fields, and responsibilities for reviews of anonymized data collections;

3. assessing and managing privacy risks, including documentation requirements to support statements about potential privacy risks in PIAs and for determinations that PIAs are not required;

4. monitoring and auditing privacy controls; and

5. documenting information security risk-assessment results consistently and comprehensively to include all NIST-recommended elements.

- To enhance the protection of collected consumer financial data, the Director of CFPB should fully implement the following five privacy and security steps:

  1. develop a comprehensive written privacy plan that brings together existing privacy policies and guidance;

  2. obtain periodic reviews of the privacy program's practices as part of the independent audit of CFPB's operations and budget;

  3. develop and implement role-based privacy training;

  4. update remedial plans for the information system that maintains consumer financial data and related components to include all identified weaknesses and realistic scheduled completion dates that reflect current priorities and available resources; and

  5. include an evaluation of compliance with contract provisions relating to information security in CFPB's review of the service provider that processes consumer financial data for CFPB.

- To provide greater assurance of compliance with PRA, the Director of CFPB should also consult further with OMB about whether PRA requirements apply to its credit card data collection and information-sharing agreement with OCC, and document the result of this consultation.

We are also making a recommendation to the Comptroller of the Currency. To ensure compliance with federal law, the Comptroller of the Currency should seek timely approval from OMB under PRA for OCC's credit card and mortgage collections, including the information-sharing agreement with CFPB for credit card data.

Agency Comments and Our Evaluation

We provided a draft of this report to CFPB, CFTC, the Consumer Product Safety Commission, FDIC, the Federal Reserve, FHFA, FTC, NCUA, OCC, OMB, SEC, and Treasury for review and comment. CFPB, OCC, and NCUA provided written comments that we reprinted in appendixes III, IV, and V, respectively. CFPB, FDIC, the Federal Reserve, FTC, OCC, and OMB provided technical comments that we incorporated, as appropriate. CFTC, the Consumer Product Safety Commission, FHFA, SEC, and Treasury did not provide comments.

In written comments, CFPB concurred with our recommendations and noted that the report provides important information about the data CFPB uses to meet its statutory responsibilities and ways that CFPB can further enhance privacy and security safeguards. CFPB further noted that other federal prudential regulators collect similar amounts of consumer financial data and discussed ways in which CFPB has been working to reduce the burden or costs to financial institutions providing the data.

CFPB outlined the actions the agency was taking or planned to take in response to our recommendations. For example, CFPB agreed to adopt formal procedures for its Data Intake Group for documenting its practices to ensure compliance with applicable requirements and consultations with OMB about PRA applicability. CFPB also noted it will develop written procedures for the de-identification of data containing personal identifiers. CFPB also agreed to review existing procedures related to its risk-assessment documentation for information security controls.

Furthermore, CFPB said it has been developing a comprehensive written privacy plan, which will discuss how the agency will assess and manage privacy risks and monitor and audit privacy controls. CFPB also plans to develop additional role-based privacy training for its staff, review its remedial action plans to ensure appropriate details are documented and remediated on schedule, and review its information security risk-management process to further refine oversight of service providers. Finally, CFPB agreed to consult with OMB again about its credit card collection.

In written comments, OCC also agreed with our recommendation to seek PRA approval from OMB for its credit card and mortgage collections. OCC noted that during the course of our review, OCC officials found that they were collecting data from more than 10 banks, which would require OMB approval under PRA. OCC noted that on September 5, 2014, it published a notice in the *Federal Register* about these collections and indicated that it planned to submit packages to OMB seeking the appropriate approval.

In its written comments, NCUA noted the importance of safeguarding consumer financial data and the role of CFPB in consumer protection.

We are sending copies of this report to the appropriate congressional committees, the Director of CFPB, the Chairman of CFTC, the Chairman of the U.S. Consumer Product Safety Commission, the Chairman of FDIC, the Chair of the Federal Reserve, the Director of FHFA, the Chairwoman of FTC, the Chairman of NCUA, the Comptroller of the Currency, the Director of OMB, the Chair of SEC, and the Secretary of the Treasury. In addition, the report is available at no charge on the GAO website at http://www.gao.gov. If you or your staff have any questions about this report, please contact me at (202) 512-8678 or clowersa@gao.gov. Contact points for our Offices of Congressional Relations and Public Affairs may be found on the last page of this report. GAO staff who made key contributions to this report are listed in appendix VI.

A. Nicole Clowers
Director
Financial Markets
and Community Investment

List of Addressees

The Honorable Tom Udall
Chairman
The Honorable Mike Johanns
Ranking Member
Subcommittee on Financial Services and General Government
Committee on Appropriations
United States Senate

The Honorable Mike Crapo
Ranking Member
Committee on Banking, Housing, and Urban Affairs
United States Senate

The Honorable Ander Crenshaw
Chairman
The Honorable José E. Serrano
Ranking Member
Subcommittee on Financial Services and General Government
Committee on Appropriations
House of Representatives

The Honorable Shelley Moore Capito
Chairman
Subcommittee on Financial Institutions and Consumer Credit
Committee on Financial Services
House of Representatives

The Honorable Carolyn B. Maloney
Ranking Member
Subcommittee on Capital Markets and Government Sponsored
Enterprises
Committee on Financial Services
House of Representatives

Appendix I: Objectives, Scope, and Methodology

The objectives of this report were to review (1) the Consumer Financial Protection Bureau's (CFPB) consumer financial data collection efforts, including the authorities, scope, purposes, and uses of these collections, and the ways in which CFPB has collaborated with other federal financial regulators as part of these collections; (2) the extent to which CFPB complied with statutory restrictions on its consumer financial data collection authorities and federal privacy requirements; and (3) the extent to which CFPB has assessed the risks of these collections and applied appropriate information security protections over these data.

To describe the authorities, scope, purposes, and uses of CFPB's data collections, we reviewed relevant portions of the Dodd-Frank Wall Street Reform and Consumer Protection Act (Dodd-Frank Act), CFPB studies, regulations, and contracts with data aggregators. Our review focused on large-scale consumer financial data collections CFPB obtained under supervisory or market monitoring authorities, as well as voluntary requests, and not data collected related to consumer complaints or for investigative or enforcement purposes. We studied 12 large-scale CFPB data collections that included consumer financial data the agency was collecting or had collected during the period from January 1, 2012 through July 1, 2014. CFPB research staff identified and confirmed that these 12 data collections represented the extent of large-scale data collections from multiple institutions being studied by CFPB staff during this time period. We excluded any planned data collections or collections under development. We focused our analysis of CFPB's data collections, studies, and examination materials on consumer financial data collections that occurred since January 2012, as CFPB had limited data collections before that time.

We physically reviewed several of CFPB's large-scale data collections on-site: consumer credit report information, credit cards, deposit advance products, overdraft fees, storefront payday loans, and private student loans. For the other large-scale collections we reviewed the data field names and descriptions: Mortgages (Corelogic contract), private-label mortgages (Blackbox Logic contract), automobile sales, online payday loans, credit scores, and arbitration case records. We did not assess the appropriateness of any individual fields for which CFPB is collecting data. We interviewed CFPB staff from the Research, Markets, and Regulation and Supervision, Fair Lending, and Enforcement teams as well as CFPB legal staff.

To describe the data collections from other prudential regulators as well as any overlap or duplication of efforts, we reviewed relevant agency

publications and interviewed officials and staff from the Board of
Governors of the Federal Reserve System (Federal Reserve), Office of
the Comptroller of the Currency (OCC), Federal Deposit Insurance
Corporation, and the National Credit Union Administration. We also
reviewed the Federal Reserve's public notifications about its collections
for conducting bank holding company stress tests (Y-14 collections),
which included notices in the *Federal Register* about its credit card and
mortgage data collections, and OCC's documents related its credit card
and mortgage data collections, including its contract with a data
aggregator. We also reviewed the large scale consumer financial data
collections of OCC, FDIC, and the Federal Reserve to determine whether
they contained information that directly identifies individuals. We did not
assess the privacy or information security controls of these collections for
this report.

We also discussed the extent to which other agencies with financial
markets or consumer regulatory responsibilities also collect consumer
information, including with staff from the Commodity Futures Trading
Commission, the Consumer Product Safety Commission, the Federal
Housing Finance Agency (FHFA), the Federal Trade Commission, and
Securities and Exchange Commission. To describe the ways in which
CFPB coordinates with other regulators on data collections, we reviewed
memorandums of understanding and information-sharing agreements
CFPB has with other federal regulators and interviewed regulatory staff.
We focused our review on the CFPB's information-sharing agreements
for large-scale data collections: one with FHFA for the National Mortgage
Database and another with OCC for the credit card database, and
interviewed relevant staff at each of these agencies about the
agreements and developments of the data sharing.

To describe what is known about the costs and benefits of CFPB's data
collections, we reviewed CFPB contracts, reports, rulemakings,
testimonies and responses to congressional questions. To learn more
about financial institutions' experiences providing consumer financial data
and how these experiences compared with other prudential regulators,
we interviewed representatives from 9 financial institutions. We randomly
selected and interviewed eight institutions that are supervised by CFPB
and that provide credit card account data to either CFPB or OCC on an
ongoing basis. We also randomly selected and interviewed 1 additional
financial institution to interview that was supervised by CFPB but does not
provide credit card data on an ongoing basis. In addition to the interviews
with representatives of these 9 institutions, we reviewed examination
workpapers from 10 randomly selected institutions. We reviewed

information requests and supervisory letters from 46 examinations at
these institutions that were completed in 2012 and 2013. We also
reviewed reports and interviewed staff from organizations that analyzed
privacy issues, monitored consumer financial topics, and served as
industry associations for financial institutions.

To determine the extent to which CFPB complied with federal data
collection requirements and privacy protections, we reviewed CFPB
privacy policies and information-sharing protocols, training requirements,
and public and nonpublic notices about collections involving personal or
direct identifiers. We compared CFPB's policies and practices against
Dodd-Frank Act requirements, Office of Management and Budget (OMB)
guidance, and recommendations of the National Institute for Standards
and Technology (NIST). We reviewed publications by the White House,
Federal Trade Commission, and other policy research organizations
about the risks for re-identification associated with collecting anonymized
consumer data. We interviewed CFPB's Chief Information Officer, Chief
Privacy Officer, and other data, research, and legal staff about their
privacy-related policies, practices, and controls implemented. We
discussed CFPB's data collections with OMB staff who review federal
collections and compliance with statutory requirements. We also spoke
with consumer and privacy advocacy groups about their views on CFPB's
data collections and with an academic expert about the extent to which
personal information can be de-anonymized.

We met with CFPB staff who analyze these data and physically observed
CFPB data collections on-site to understand the scope of the data
collections and how CFPB treated any personally identifying information.
We reviewed the data fields for each of the 12 databases under review.
For 3 of the 12 databases, CFPB stores the data at the institution level.
For these databases (payday lending, overdraft fees, and deposit
advance products), we reviewed a sample of seven of the institutions that
provided data. We took steps to ensure the accuracy of key information
used in this report, including interviewing agency officials, obtaining
original source documents, and physically observing database contents
on-site when necessary. We determined the data were reliable for the
purposes used in this report, specifically giving readers an estimate of the
number of records in each dataset.

To describe the adequacy and effectiveness of CFPB's information
security protections, we reviewed CFPB's security policies and
procedures for the information system and related components that store
consumer financial data. We compared CFPB's current information

security policies and procedures against the NIST risk-assessment framework, which emphasizes the selection, implementation, and monitoring of security controls, and the authorization of information systems. We reviewed and analyzed documentation and policies related to CFPB's system security plan, risk assessments, security assessment reports, and remedial action plans and compared each against applicable NIST and CFPB-defined standards. We evaluated the extent to which CFPB has established and implemented policies and procedures to ensure its service providers provide adequate security protections over the consumer financial data which is collected and maintained on its behalf. This was done by reviewing and analyzing documentation of CFPB's evaluation of a service provider and comparing it against CFBP requirements. We reviewed prior audit work conducted by the Inspector General for the Federal Reserve and CFPB in this area. We interviewed the Chief Information Officer, Chief Information Security Officer, and other CFPB staff about these policies, procedures, and reports. We reviewed logical access controls for the information system component in which CFPB stores and analyzes consumer financial data. We reviewed and observed access control lists, authentication and account management, server administration and configuration, firewall technology, and vulnerability and compliance scanning. We also interviewed the CFPB staff who manage these servers about these controls.

We conducted this performance audit from August 2013 to August 2014 in accordance with generally accepted government auditing standards. Those standards require that we plan and perform the audit to obtain sufficient, appropriate evidence to provide a reasonable basis for our findings and conclusions based on our audit objectives. We believe that the evidence obtained provides a reasonable basis for our findings and conclusions based on our audit objectives.

Appendix II: List of Reports CFPB Prepared Using Collected Consumer Financial Data, as of July 15, 2014

Report title	Date of publication	Origin of report	Purpose	Use of consumer financial data
Private Student Loans	August 29, 2012	Mandate under the Dodd-Frank Act	To describe the market for private student loans and related consumer protection issues	Loan-level origination information for all educational loans of nine major lenders for all loans that originated from 2005 through 2011. Analysis of the number of loan originations and their associated interest rates.
Analysis of Differences between Consumer- and Creditor-Purchased Credit Scores	September 2012	Mandate under the Dodd-Frank Act	To compare credit scores sold to creditors (lenders) and those sold to consumers by nationwide credit reporting agencies and determine whether differences between those scores disadvantage consumers.	Random sample of 200,000 consumer credit reports from each of three nationwide credit reporting agencies. Zip code and age information allowed comparison of scores by consumer demographics.
Payday Loans and Deposit Advance Products: A White Paper of Initial Data Findings	April 24, 2013	CFPB-initiated	To understand the payday loan and deposit advance product market and present facts related to CFPB's analysis of these markets.	Sample of account- and loan- level data from five to nine storefront payday lenders and some depository institutions providing deposit advance products.
CFPB Study of Overdraft Programs: A White Paper of Initial Data Findings	June 2013	CFPB-initiated	To understand financial institutions' overdraft programs for consumer checking accounts.	Sample of consumer checking account and transaction data from a sample of large depository institutions.
The CARD Act Report: A Review of the Impact of the CARD Act on the Consumer Credit Market	October 1, 2013	Mandate under Credit Card Accountability Responsibility and Disclosure Act (CARD Act) of 2009[a]	To review the consumer credit card market and the effect of the CARD Act on the cost and availability of credit and the adequacy of protections relating to credit card plans.	Credit card account data provided by financial institutions submitting data to CFPB and OCC.
Arbitration Study Preliminary Results: Section 1028(a) Study Results to Date	December 12, 2013	Mandate under the Dodd-Frank Act	To provide preliminary results on the use of pre-dispute arbitration contract provisions in consumer financial products or services.	More than 1,000 arbitration case records from the American Arbitration Association from January 2010 through 2012. Sample of consumer credit records from CFPB's Consumer Credit Panel.
CFPB Data Point: Payday Lending	March 2014	CFPB-initiated	To describe patterns of consumer borrowing after the consumer obtains a payday loan and use of consumer loan products.	Same sample of data described in the April 2013 report above on payday loans and deposit advances.
Data Point: Medical Debt and Credit Scores	May 2014	CFPB-initiated	To review the use of medical debt collections in credit scoring models.	Sample of consumer credit files from CFPB's Consumer Credit Panel.
Report on the Use of Remittance Histories in Credit Scoring	July 2014	CFPB-initiated follow-up to mandate under the Dodd-Frank Act	To discuss empirical research about whether data on remittance transfers can enhance the credit scores of consumers.	Random sample of consumer records, provided by a large remittance transfer provider and matched with credit records, as well as a control sample of randomly selected credit records.

Source: GAO analysis of CFPB information. | GAO-14-758

[a]The CARD Act originally directed the Federal Reserve to complete the biennial report, but the Dodd-Frank Act transferred this authority to CFPB.

Appendix III: Comments from the Consumer Financial Protection Bureau

1700 G Street NW, Washington, DC 20552

September 3, 2014

Ms. A. Nicole Clowers
Director, Financial Markets and Community Investment
U.S. Government Accountability Office
441 G Street, NW
Washington, DC 20548

Dear Ms. Clowers:

Thank you for the opportunity to comment on the Government Accountability Office's (GAO) draft report, GAO-14-758. We greatly appreciate GAO's consultation and collaboration with the Consumer Financial Protection Bureau (Bureau) over the course of its year-long review and believe the report provides important information about the Bureau's statutory responsibilities; its collection, use, and protection of information needed to carry out these responsibilities; and steps the Bureau can take to further enhance existing safeguards.

GAO's objectives for this engagement were to review the Bureau's authority to collect consumer financial data, its purpose for and use of that data, and its efforts to protect this information from unauthorized disclosure. As GAO notes in its report, access to such data allows the Bureau to "better detect risks in consumer financial markets and improve federal oversight of consumer financial ... laws." The Bureau's commitment to minimizing risks inherent in data collection is reflected in GAO's finding that the Bureau "has taken steps to assess the risks posed by these data and implemented controls or taken other actions to address the risks."

The Dodd-Frank Wall Street Reform and Consumer Protection Act (Dodd-Frank Act), which created the Bureau, directs the Bureau "to implement and . . . enforce Federal consumer financial law" so as to "ensur[e] that all consumers have access to markets for consumer financial products and services and that [such] markets ... are fair, transparent, and

1

competitive."[1] To make certain that the Bureau carries out statutorily mandated supervisory and enforcement activities with a thorough understanding of the markets it oversees, the Dodd-Frank Act established the Bureau's authorities for, among other things, "collecting, researching, monitoring, and publishing information relevant to the functioning of markets for consumer financial products and services."[2]

As GAO emphasizes in its report, prior to the creation of the Bureau "and during the 2007-2009 financial crisis, [GAO] and others noted that the lack of data on consumer financial products and services hindered federal oversight in areas such as mortgages and fair lending." This recognition by GAO and others serves as a crucial reminder that failing to ensure that financial regulators have access to sound data about the markets they oversee can have devastating results for consumers and the economy.

Information received by the Bureau and reviewed by GAO in this engagement has been used, as intended by the Dodd-Frank Act, to inform the Bureau's rulemakings, supervise covered persons and service providers, and enforce Federal consumer financial law. The Bureau also has discharged its statutory obligation to analyze such information and to report the results of that analysis to Congress and the public. In its review, GAO highlights several Bureau reports that drew heavily on analysis of consumer financial information, including the Bureau's reports on *Private Student Loans, Analysis of Differences between Consumer-and-Creditor Purchased Credit Scores*, and the *CARD Act Report*.[3]

Recognizing, as GAO does in its report, that the federal prudential regulators collect consumer financial data on a scale similar to that of the Bureau, the Bureau seeks to coordinate and streamline data collections through several efforts outlined by GAO. Such efforts include information-sharing agreements with fellow regulators, coordinated examination scheduling, collecting data samples where such methods allow for reliable analysis and will not result in additional burden or cost to institutions, and proactively seeking information from supervised entities about potential

---

[1] 12 U.S.C. § 5511(a), Pub. L. 111-203, Title X, § 1021(a) (July 21, 2010).
[2] 12 U.S.C. § 5511(c), Pub. L. 111-203, Title X, § 1021(c) (July 21, 2010).
[3] Available at http://www.consumerfinance.gov/reports/.

2

overlap in collections. As the Bureau's supervision program matures and its relationships with supervised entities—some of which have never been subject to federal oversight—develop, we expect to see further reductions in the complexity and/or burden of Bureau data requests, and we are gratified that the majority of the institutions GAO interviewed are already noticing these changes.

We concur with the recommendations addressed to the Bureau in the report. These recommendations focus primarily on documentation of processes and procedures related to data collection and protection. GAO acknowledges several important steps the Bureau has already taken to record, implement, and enhance existing data privacy and security measures. These steps include adopting privacy policies, issuing public notices of information collection, completing privacy impact assessments, creating a framework for data sensitivity classification, and adopting an Information Governance Policy establishing agency-wide principles for receipt, management, and disclosure of information. These and other efforts reflect a Bureau-wide commitment to building a data governance structure that is both effective and sustainable.

Regarding GAO's specific recommendations, the Bureau has already taken or plans to take the following steps:

- *To help ensure consistent implementation of its current processes and practices, the Director of CFPB should establish or enhance written procedures for:*

    1. *the data intake process, including reviews of proposed data collections for compliance [with]applicable legal requirements and restrictions and documentation requirements for consultations with OMB about PRA applicability;*

Since early 2013, the Bureau's Data Intake Group (DIG) has reviewed proposed data collections for compliance with the Dodd-Frank Act, the Paperwork Reduction Act (PRA), the Privacy Act, and other applicable laws and policies. The DIG includes representatives from the Legal Division, PRA Office, and Privacy Office, along with other relevant experts from offices across the Bureau. By establishing the

3

DIG, the Bureau has formalized review and collaboration with
respect to data collection.

DIG members convene formal meetings to review proposals to collect
new data. The Bureau's Chief Information Officer (CIO) must
approve any recommendation by the DIG before a proposed
collection proceeds.

In addition, the Data Governance Board (DGB), established by the
Bureau's Information Governance Policy and comprised of senior
Bureau staff with relevant expertise, advises the CIO on data intake
and related policies and procedures. With the DIG, the DGB, and the
Information Governance Policy, the Bureau has put in place robust
policies and practices to ensure that collection of consumer financial
information and other data is accompanied by appropriate
safeguards, as recommended by GAO.

Reflecting its commitment to continually update and enhance the
Bureau's internal controls, the Bureau is also drafting formal
procedures for documenting existing DIG practices. These formal
procedures will include documenting the Bureau's reviews of
proposed data collections for compliance with applicable laws and
developing documentation requirements for consultations with OMB
about PRA applicability. These enhanced procedures will ensure
that the Bureau consistently manages and documents compliance
with respect to its data intake activities.

> 2. *anonymizing data, including how staff should assess data sensitivity;
> which steps to take to anonymize data fields, and responsibilities for
> reviews of anonymized data collections;*

Whenever appropriate, the Bureau collects data that is stripped of
direct personal identifiers. GAO has correctly noted that the majority
of the large datasets maintained by the Bureau do not contain direct
personal identifiers.

When it is necessary for the Bureau to receive data that contain
direct personal identifiers, the Bureau protects this information by

4

employing a variety of measures, including physical access controls, source masking, and de-identifying data when appropriate. The Bureau is also developing standards by which staff should assess data sensitivity.

To ensure that de-identification procedures are consistently applied across the Bureau, the Bureau is also developing written procedures that will formalize existing practices regarding de-identification. These procedures will define roles and responsibilities for de-identification, specify the steps to take in the de-identification process, and establish a process for reviews of de-identified data collections.

3. *assessing and managing privacy risks, including documentation requirements to support statements about potential privacy risks in PIAs and for determinations that PIAs are not required;*

This recommendation is addressed below in response to GAO's recommendation for a comprehensive written privacy plan.

4. *monitoring and auditing privacy controls; and*

This recommendation is addressed below in response to GAO's recommendation for a comprehensive written privacy plan.

5. *documenting information security risk-assessment results consistently and comprehensively to include all NIST-recommended elements.*

As noted by GAO, the Bureau's information security program includes a risk management process that aligns to the steps of the NIST Risk Management Framework, including security categorization, security control selection, security control implementation, security control assessment, information system authorization, and security control monitoring. In execution of this process, Bureau systems are categorized and security controls designed and implemented according to the sensitivity of the data to be stored and processed therein. We appreciate GAO's

5

acknowledgement of existing actions by the Bureau to provide
necessary security protections and incorporate NIST-recommended
elements.

Risk assessments are performed and documented so as to present
decision makers with pertinent system and risk data, facilitating
efficient and holistic risk-based decisions to authorize systems for
use. With respect to risk assessments and other areas of information
security, the Bureau evaluates and implements NIST guidance and
recommendations in a manner that assures levels of data security
equal to the associated risk. The Bureau appreciates the
recommendations provided by GAO and has already begun to review
standing procedures noting opportunities to incorporate suggested
NIST content and format changes for risk assessment reports.

- *To enhance the protections of collected consumer financial data, the*
  Director of CFPB should fully implement the following five privacy and
  security steps:

  1. *develop comprehensive written privacy plan that brings together*
     existing privacy policies and guidance;

The Bureau's Privacy Office is in the process of building on and
consolidating existing privacy policies, guidance, and protections to
formalize the Bureau's privacy program and develop a
comprehensive written privacy plan. The plan will include written
procedures for assessing and managing privacy risks, including
documentation requirements to support statements about potential
privacy risks in Privacy Impact Assessments (PIAs) and for
determinations that PIAs are not required. Notably, the Bureau has
already developed and approved a Bureau-wide policy on PIAs,
which will be incorporated into the Bureau's privacy plan. The plan
also will address auditing of privacy controls.

  2. *obtain periodic reviews of the privacy program's practices as part of*
     the independent audit of CFPB's operations and budget;

6

The Privacy Office has participated in a number of audits since the Bureau was formed. These audits include the 2012 Independent Performance Audit of CFPB Operations and Budget, the 2013 Assessment of Internal Privacy and Security Controls for the Consumer Response System, a review of Corrective Actions in 2013 related to the 2012 Annual Independent Audit, and the current GAO audit. The Bureau's plans to complete a comprehensive written privacy plan will include procedures for obtaining and monitoring auditing of privacy controls.

3. *develop and implement role-based privacy training;*

The Bureau has already developed and provided role-based privacy training for the Offices of Research and Consumer Response and is developing role-based training for other Bureau offices. The Privacy Office also provides training to new hires, and the Bureau requires annual training for current employees covering the essentials of privacy requirements and expectations. The training includes information about each individual's responsibilities and requirements for protecting personally identifiable information, compliance procedures for safeguarding sensitive information, limiting access to information, and reporting potential incidents.

4. *Update remedial plans for the information system that maintains consumer financial data and related components to include all identified weaknesses and realistic scheduled completion dates that reflect current priorities and available resources; and*

We appreciate GAO's recognition of information security protections the Bureau has put in place, including adopting the NIST recommended framework to manage risk, establishing access controls for protecting consumer information, and the development of a robust information security program. The GAO's findings in this respect add to similar recognition in recent audits by the Inspector General that commended a number of steps the Bureau has taken to secure its technology and data in accordance with FISMA requirements.

7

The Bureau's information security program includes a comprehensive risk management process that aligns to the NIST Risk Management Framework. The Bureau's information security program and associated processes provide effective controls to afford the appropriate level of protection to Bureau data. By integrating pertinent guidance and best practices from government and industry, the Bureau's information security program efficiently and effectively discovers, mitigates, and manages risk to the Bureau.

Mindful of the nature of rapidly evolving technology, and equally dynamic threats to the same, the Bureau constantly monitors for vulnerabilities and weaknesses. When this monitoring identifies weaknesses, the Bureau records the weaknesses in a remedial action plan, rates them according to the associated risk, assigns a completion date, and manages to remediation. The Bureau manages these remedial action plans appropriately: to mitigate risk, improve security, and continuously refine the CFPB IT program. The Bureau allocates its limited resources so as to most effectively address potential risks by prioritizing remedial actions addressed to greatest risks and/or that provide the greatest return. As an example, GAO reviewed a system remediation plan that was leveraged effectively to drive enterprise-wide standardization of secure configuration baselines, thereby improving the Bureau's security posture and technology management operations.

The Bureau will continue to refine its remedial action plans and the guiding process to ensure that plans contain the appropriate level of detail and remediation actions are afforded the appropriate priority and resources to remediate on schedule.

> 5. *include an evaluation of compliance with contract provisions relating to information security in CFPB's review of the service provider that processes consumer financial data for CFPB.*

We appreciate the recommendation and are reviewing the standing information security risk management process to identify opportunities for refinement. The Bureau understands the importance of providing proper oversight and evaluations of its

8

contracted service providers. The Bureau has established a number of policies, processes, and controls to ensure that the information security program and contract oversight functions achieve and maintain visibility into the contractor's operations.

The Bureau has established a variety of mechanisms to evaluate and monitor its contractors, and calibrates its evaluations and monitoring by considering the inherent risk of the contracted service. The Bureau applies a graduated scale of contractor assessment, based on the NIST-recommended practice of *test-once, use-many* in which past assessments of similar scope are used to support limited testing for specific purposes to provide the Bureau with an accurate risk-profile for the service provider. For example, the particular service provider risk assessment analyzed by GAO included an evaluation of the service provider's independent risk assessment, the contracted service, pertinent controls and control activities, and a review of the service provider's business operations. That risk assessment resulted in a single recommendation not related to a system or provider weakness, but rather for a specific improvement to Bureau operations and oversight, which is being addressed through the Bureau's Data Intake Group. This recommendation was not documented in the remedial action plan for the service provider, but rather carried forward by the Bureau's CIO as a part of agency-wide data governance efforts noted previously in this letter.

- *To provide greater assurance of compliance with PRA, the Director of CFPB should consult further with OMB about whether PRA requirements apply to its credit card data collection and information-sharing agreement with OCC, and document the results of this consultation.*

As noted in GAO's report, the Bureau has already consulted with OMB regarding the collection of credit card data. To ensure compliance with applicable privacy and related protections for data collection, the Bureau has put in place a Data Intake Group (DIG) to conduct necessary legal, cybersecurity, and privacy reviews, including review of applicable PRA requirements. The Bureau's efforts to formalize the DIG's procedures are underway. As recommended, the Bureau

9

will consult again with OMB about whether PRA requirements apply
to the Bureau's collection of certain credit card data and the Bureau
will document this further consultation.

We look forward to continuing to work with GAO as it assesses Bureau
progress in implementing these recommendations and in future reviews.

The Bureau is committed to ensuring fair and consistent application of
Federal consumer financial laws, and to responsible collection and
protection of the data necessary to fulfill that statutory obligation. To that
end, we appreciate GAO's efforts throughout this engagement to develop a
comprehensive and balanced understanding of the Bureau's authority to
collect consumer financial information, as well as the purposes underlying
its use and the risks and necessary safeguards associated with receipt of
such information.

Sincerely,

Richard Cordray

Richard Cordray
Director

10

Appendix IV: Comments from the Office of the Comptroller of the Currency

 Office of the Comptroller of the Currency

Washington, DC 20219

September 9, 2014

Ms. A. Nicole Clowers
Director, Financial Markets and Community Investment
United States Government Accountability Office
Washington, DC 20548

Dear Ms. Clowers:

The Office of the Comptroller of the Currency (OCC) has received and reviewed the Government Accountability Office's (GAO) draft report titled "Consumer Financial Protection Bureau (CFPB) Privacy and Security Controls for Data Collections Should Be Enhanced." This report addresses the CFPB's collection of consumer financial information and its compliance with certain requirements in Federal law, including requirements pertaining to privacy and information security, and makes a number of recommendations to the CFPB for further action on these matters.

In addition, the report includes one recommendation to the OCC. Specifically, the GAO recommends that the OCC seek timely approval from the Office of Management and Budget (OMB) under the Paperwork Reduction Act (PRA) for OCC's credit card, mortgage, and home equity line of credit (HELOC) data collection programs, including the information-sharing agreement with the CFPB for credit card data.

In response to this recommendation, the OCC will seek OMB approval under the PRA for its credit card, mortgage, and HELOC data collection programs. Under the PRA, agencies must obtain OMB approval when collecting data from 10 or more entities. When the OCC initiated these programs, it planned to collect data from fewer than 10 banks. During the course of the GAO review, the OCC conducted its own review of its credit card, mortgage, and HELOC data collection programs and determined that there were more than 10 data reporters in each program – 16 credit card, 61 mortgage, and 64 HELOC reporters.

On September 5, 2014, pursuant to the PRA, the OCC published notices in the *Federal Register* for these data collection programs that invite public comment for 60 days. Subsequently, the OCC will submit information clearance packages to the OMB for approval of the data collection programs and anticipates that the OMB would clear the information collections by January 2015.

In addition to our response to the GAO's recommendation, we also have provided comments on the draft report at pages 21, 27, and 28. We appreciate this opportunity to review the draft report. If you need additional information, please contact Karen Solomon, Deputy Chief Counsel, (202)-649-5400.

Sincerely,

Thomas J. Curry
Comptroller of the Currency

2

Appendix V: Comments from the National Credit Union Administration

 ─────National Credit Union Administration─────────

August 28, 2014

A. Nicole Clowers
Director, Financial Markets and Community Investment
United States Government Accountability Office
441 G Street, NW
Washington, DC 20548

Dear Ms. Clowers:

Thank you for the opportunity to review and comment on the Government Accountability Office (GAO) report entitled, *Consumer Financial Protection Bureau: Privacy and Security Controls for Data Collection Should Be Enhanced* (GAO-14-758). This report addresses the Consumer Financial Protection Bureau's (CFPB) collection of consumer financial data, as well as information security controls and practices in place to protect such data.

The National Credit Union Administration understands the importance of protecting consumer financial data. We also understand the critical role CFPB serves in protecting the rights of consumers by evaluating market conditions, examining regulated institutions, and implementing appropriate rulemakings. The recommendations provided by GAO are designed to enhance efforts to protect and secure consumer financial data. We appreciate the opportunity to comment on the report.

Sincerely,

Mark A. Treichel
Executive Director

1775 Duke Street - Alexandria, VA 22314-3428 - 703-518-6300

Appendix VI: GAO Contact and Staff Acknowledgments

GAO Contact	A. Nicole Clowers, (202) 512-8678 or clowersa@gao.gov
Staff Acknowledgments	In addition to the contact named above, Cody Goebel (Assistant Director), Katherine Bittinger Eikel (Analyst-in-Charge), Edward R. Alexander, Jr., Rachel Batkins, Don Brown, William Chatlos, West Coile, Nathan Gottfried, Fatima Jahan, Anjalique Lawrence, Bryan Maculloch, Marc Molino, Patricia Moye, David Plocher, Barbara Roesmann, Maria Stattel, Anne Stevens, Shaunyce Wallace, and Heneng Yu made significant contributions to this report.

GAO's Mission	The Government Accountability Office, the audit, evaluation, and investigative arm of Congress, exists to support Congress in meeting its constitutional responsibilities and to help improve the performance and accountability of the federal government for the American people. GAO examines the use of public funds; evaluates federal programs and policies; and provides analyses, recommendations, and other assistance to help Congress make informed oversight, policy, and funding decisions. GAO's commitment to good government is reflected in its core values of accountability, integrity, and reliability.
Obtaining Copies of GAO Reports and Testimony	The fastest and easiest way to obtain copies of GAO documents at no cost is through GAO's website (http://www.gao.gov). Each weekday afternoon, GAO posts on its website newly released reports, testimony, and correspondence. To have GAO e-mail you a list of newly posted products, go to http://www.gao.gov and select "E-mail Updates."
Order by Phone	The price of each GAO publication reflects GAO's actual cost of production and distribution and depends on the number of pages in the publication and whether the publication is printed in color or black and white. Pricing and ordering information is posted on GAO's website, http://www.gao.gov/ordering.htm. Place orders by calling (202) 512-6000, toll free (866) 801-7077, or TDD (202) 512-2537. Orders may be paid for using American Express, Discover Card, MasterCard, Visa, check, or money order. Call for additional information.
Connect with GAO	Connect with GAO on Facebook, Flickr, Twitter, and YouTube. Subscribe to our RSS Feeds or E-mail Updates. Listen to our Podcasts. Visit GAO on the web at www.gao.gov.
To Report Fraud, Waste, and Abuse in Federal Programs	Contact: Website: http://www.gao.gov/fraudnet/fraudnet.htm E-mail: fraudnet@gao.gov Automated answering system: (800) 424-5454 or (202) 512-7470
Congressional Relations	Katherine Siggerud, Managing Director, siggerudk@gao.gov, (202) 512-4400, U.S. Government Accountability Office, 441 G Street NW, Room 7125, Washington, DC 20548
Public Affairs	Chuck Young, Managing Director, youngc1@gao.gov, (202) 512-4800 U.S. Government Accountability Office, 441 G Street NW, Room 7149 Washington, DC 20548

Please Print on Recycled Paper.